Exiles in Hollywood

# Exiles in Hollywood

David Wallace

Limelight Editions

Published in 2006 by Limelight Editions
512 Newark Pompton Turnpike
Pompton Plains, New Jersey 07444

The photographs in this book are reproduced by permission and courtesy of the following:

Bison Archives: pages xviii, 32, 58, 82, 88, 124, 134, 142, 148, 154, 174, 184, 198, 208, 210, 218, 225, 228

Feuchtwanger Memorial Library, Specialized Libraries and Archival Collections, University of Southern California: pages 66, 74, 96, 105, 110, 166

Photofest: pages 14, 21, 116, 191, 205

Alma (www.alma-mahler.at): page 42

For quotation of the poems "Garden in Progress" and "Hollywood" from *Poems 1913–1956* by Bertolt Brecht, gratitude is expressed to Methuen Publishing Ltd.

For quotation of the poem "This is a house of art" by Norman Corwin, gratitude is expressed to Norman Corwin.

While every effort has been made to trace copyright holders and obtain permission, this has not been possible in all cases; any omissions brought to our attention will be remedied in future editions.

Library of Congress Cataloging-in-Publication Data is available upon request.

ISBN 0-8791-032-99

Printed in the United States of America
Book design by Snow Creative Services

www.limelighteditions.com

For Chris

# Contents

# Introduction

To paraphrase a famous line from Charles Dickens's *A Tale of Two Cities*, the 1930s and 1940s were, for millions, the worst of times. But, for a lucky few, they would become—at least comparatively speaking—the best of times.

Worldwide economic depression and the tragic turmoil of a world war terrorized everyone. But worst off were the thousands of artists, musicians, playwrights, philosophers, architects, and filmmakers living in Germany, Austria, and France who were persecuted for their faiths, their ethnicity, and often for their very art and craft. Many, most of them Jews, would die in concentration camps. But more than a few survived by fleeing their homelands for neutral Switzerland, Great Britain, and the United States. And, despite the tragic reasons for their collective exodus, astonishingly, for a surprising number of these refugees—among them many of the greatest creative talents of the twentieth century—the subsequent years spent in new, adopted homelands would be counted among the best years of their lives.

Somewhat oddly (certainly unexpectedly), the new home chosen by most participants in what would be the greatest immigration in history of intellectual and creative talent wasn't a cultural center like New York or London. It was a metropolis then and now often dismissed as a cultural wasteland. But for a great part of the late 1930s and 1940s, the presence of such talent as composers Igor Stravinsky, Arnold Schoenberg, and Sergei Rachmaninoff; architects like Berlin's Rudolf Schindler and Vienna's Richard Neutra; writers like Thomas Mann and Franz Werfel; and filmmakers like Billy Wilder, Fritz Lang, and Jean Renoir made that "wasteland" a cultural capital—the Athens of

America: Los Angeles. The effect of it all is still with us in many of the books we read, in much of the music we hear, certainly in many of the films we watch, and in some ways how we view the world today. Many of the refugees discovered that instead of being exiled to a culturally barren desert, as some suspected, they had been, to quote the refugee composer Arnold Schoenberg, "driven into paradise." Unlike classical Athens, whose name is often invoked as the avatar of the enlightened, intellectually driven community, this modern Athens, paradise or otherwise, endured for less than two decades.

Although the reality of Los Angeles becoming a cultural Mecca was surprising (many people today, of course, still refuse to believe the place ever was or ever will be anything but La-La-Land), the idea itself wasn't exactly new. In fact, long before the European intellectual immigrants began arriving, some local movers and shakers actually decided to create an "Athens of the West" beside Santa Monica Bay. Attracted by the weather, some European émigrés had already chosen Southern California as their home years before refugees from the Nazis began arriving. "I came to California for the first time in 1927," said Bruno Walter, a conductor whose name is today legend. "I had to conduct a concert at the Hollywood Bowl, and fell in love with the place at first sight," Walter added. "After that I always wanted to make my domicile here, but only in 1935 could I do so." By then he hardly had a choice: as a Jew already in America, he certainly would have been disinclined to move back to his native Germany. But why California instead of New York, then the center of America's classical music-making? Like many other less creatively endowed European immigrants already in Southern California, he was also fleeing "the *allegro furioso* of New York City to the *allegretto grazioso* of Beverly Hills." The weather was better.

When Mr. Hitler began deciding who was and who was not worthy of being a citizen of the thousand-year Reich, the migration to Southern California exploded like the Oklahoma land rush of the 1860s. Amazingly, it has been estimated that during this time half of *all* the European intellectual and creative talent moved to this relatively small patch of California's coast. And four-fifths of that was German-speaking.

Some émigrés, like Charles Laughton, Alfred Hitchcock, Charles Chaplin, Greta Garbo, and Marlene Dietrich, had come earlier to make films. But, in the 1930s and early 1940s, most came to escape Nazi persecution. "It was a mass migration of a thrown-together elite unprecedented in history," says Hollywood Bowl Museum director Dr. Carol Merrill-Mirsky.

Their arrival changed many things—but the most enduring change was to the movies—America's great cultural product. By hybridizing the new, gritty novel style perhaps best epitomized by the crime novels of Raymond Chandler, James M. Cain, and their contemporaries with the nihilistic cultural ambiance of Berlin and the Weimar Republic, where so many of the new arrivals trained, a major film style evolved—ironically in Los Angeles, the sunniest of film locales—we call it film noir.

The beginnings of the style had already been pioneered by Austrian émigré Erich von Stroheim in his American film *Greed* (1925) followed by 1927's *The Wedding March.* In them, von Stroheim introduced elements drawn from German naturalism and expressionism and from Austrian fin de siécle *weltschmertz.* They included the naturalistic precision of details in settings by means of camera technique, depiction of abject poverty (hitherto a relatively rare theme in American films), ironic portrayals of materialistic and erotic desires of both the nobility and the bourgeoisie, pacifism as the ideal in the struggle over the future of humanity. Of course, such socially engaged themes had been employed before in American films, but only fitfully in movies by such directors as Chaplin and D. W. Griffith. But von Stroheim's social criticism and his sarcastic representation of social decadence, including the contrast between sexual greed and true love, would have been impossible without the theories of naturalism and the theories of his fellow Austrian Sigmund Freud, combined with, eventually, the

Berlin film style. And as the fifteen hundred or so German-speaking refugees and émigrés who would eventually make their living within the film industry brought that cultural *weltanschauung* along with their resumes, what might otherwise have been a footnote to Southern California's cultural history became, in fact, an event of extreme importance to the entire American film industry.

Many, like refugees everywhere, came with few possessions and little money in their pockets. Billy Wilder, for example, newly arrived from Germany during the Christmas season of 1935, lived for a time in an anteroom outside the women's toilets in the basement of the Chateau Marmont Hotel. Refugees arrived from France, too, including filmmakers René Clair, Max Ophuls, and Jean Renoir.

The trailblazing architects Rudolf M. Schindler and Richard Neutra were also in Hollywood, creating some of what are still among the world's most architecturally advanced homes and buildings as they changed our very ideas of what a home or an office could be. The Russian-American sculptor Alexander Archipenko had earlier come to Hollywood, where he opened an art school. An acting school was opened by the famed German stage director Max Reinhardt, co-founder of the Salzburg Festival, who staged a legendary production of Shakespeare's *A Midsummer Night's Dream* at the Hollywood Bowl. Later made into a film, the production starred the young actors Mickey Rooney and Olivia de Havilland; the ten days of performances attracted more than two hundred thousand people.

In 1937, five years after publication of his most famous book, the bitterly satiric *Brave New World*, Aldous Huxley came to Hollywood, where he would write several more books, as well as screenplays, including MGM's *Pride and Prejudice* (1940).

Also among the exiles and émigrés were several of the greatest musicians and composers the twentieth century has produced. Among them: Sergei Rachmaninoff and Igor Stravinsky, along with modernists Arnold Schoenberg, George Antheil, and Ernst Krenek, the aforementioned Bruno Walter, and Otto Klemperer, who from

1933 to 1939 was music director of the Los Angeles Philharmonic (Klemperer's son, Werner, became an actor whose most famous role was playing a comedic Nazi prison camp commander on television's *Hogan's Heroes*. As they say: "Only in Hollywood . . ."). Also arriving from Vienna was the once "wunderkind" of music, Erich Wolfgang Korngold, who became hugely successful composing film music.

The greatest violinist in the world, Jascha Heifetz, virtually lived in Los Angeles during this time; he wasn't exactly a refugee, but was drawn to Los Angeles by the synergy of the place and, like many, the weather. So, too, pianists Vladimir Horowitz and Arthur Rubinstein.

Writers seemed to be everywhere on the semitropical turf. Thomas Mann, his brother Heinrich, and Bertolt Brecht, the "German Shakespeare," were here. Lion Feuchtwanger, the man who essentially created the historical novel, arrived with his wife Marta in 1941, after having been charged earlier with "premature antifascism" for a novel he wrote satirizing Hitler before the *Reichskanzler* assumed power. Writer Christopher Isherwood (whose *Berlin Diaries*, a memoir of that city's between-the-wars decadence, was eventually made into the movie *I Am a Camera,* later adapted as the musical *Cabaret)* settled in Hollywood in 1939, eventually renting a room above émigré screenwriter Salka Viertel's garage in Santa Monica. And, of course, Franz Werfel soon arrived; his novel *The Song of Bernadette* would be made into an Oscar-winning film.

Lording over it all—at least in her own mind—was Werfel's wife, Alma, the widow of composer Gustav Mahler, divorced wife of Bauhaus founder Walter Gropius, and onetime mistress of expressionist painter Oskar Kokoschka.

It wasn't an easy move for many of the new arrivals—no such assimilation of cultures is accomplished without a clash of cultures and countless misunderstandings. A perfect example is that experienced by Gottfried Reinhardt, son of the director, who was inducted into the U.S. Army in 1942. As he was on his way to Camp Crowder, Missouri, he was in the dining car visiting with actor Jack Oakie, who just happened to be on the same train, when an officer (who clearly had too much to drink) heard his accent and challenged Reinhardt's patriotism. "Who was the last president you voted for?" he demanded of the refugee. Reinhardt said, "Hindenburg, sir."

The thousands of new arrivals also missed their homes—especially the German-speaking refugees who were conflicted between their hatred of the Nazi regime and their love of the German cultural heritage as exemplified by such immortal talents as Bach, Beethoven, and Goethe. To maintain some semblance of continuity, they often gathered socially among themselves and with other transplanted persons. Many—like Billy Wilder—became fabulously successful. Others, like Bertolt Brecht, never found true financial security in their new homeland. Nevertheless, the result was a synthesis of talents and cultures that created in the City of the Angels a rare and—as it turned out—transitory time out of mind.

Living in Los Angeles then was far different then than now. There was only one freeway, the Pasadena (then called the Arroyo Seco Parkway), and that only recently opened. In contrast, there existed the finest public transportation system in the country—probably the best that ever existed in America: the Pacific Electric Railway Company and its then famous Red Cars. It was only one part—albeit the largest, with 1,105 miles of track—of a huge urban transit system that crisscrossed the Los Angeles Basin, reaching from the ocean at Santa Monica sixty miles to the orange groves of San Bernardino. Oh, yes, although they were disappearing from their ubiquitousness during the early years of the twentieth century, there were still orange groves, and lemon and grapefruit groves as well.

Life was less comfortable than today. Air-conditioning was more or less limited to theaters and some public buildings; there were no malls and few supermarkets. The diet was also far different in those days, heavy on the carbohydrates and, even in Los Angeles, relatively light on vegetables and fruit.

There was no television—at least for the general public. Personal computers and the Internet were far beyond imagining, as were such things as the compact disc and cell phones (although the technology that would enable the cell phone was invented in the early 1940s by, of all people, a Hollywood film beauty).

Home entertainment was largely limited to social get-togethers (charades was first popularized then), and home music was limited to playing heavy, breakable 78 rpm records on low-fi equipment, listening to the radio (which then broadcast a major diet of classical and popular music), or making your own music by playing a piano (so prevalent was a piano as part of the home furnishings of the era that home design in the 1930s and '40s usually reserved a designated place for the instrument, creating a bit of a headache for restorers of older homes today, who if they don't have a piano, need to figure out what to do with the space).

The radio was also vitally important for most of the refugees and émigrés, who would gather around regular and shortwave instruments at all hours of the night to hear the latest news from Europe, often wondering how their relatives back home were faring.

Why did it all end? By the 1950s, with the pain of war fading, many moved away to places they felt more congenial (for example, Alma Mahler to New York in 1952; her husband died in 1945); some, like Arnold Schoenberg, died (1951); others, like Thomas Mann, moved away in disgust as the McCarthy years, with their witch-hunts, evolved. So, too, did Richard Neutra, who began to lose profitable architectural commissions when dubbed a "socialist." Bertolt Brecht was summoned to testify before the House Un-American Activities Committee in 1947 (Congressman Richard Nixon was a member) and immediately thereafter returned to his homeland in disgust.

This, then, is the story of a people and—for all its shortcomings—the place where, for a time, thousands of European exiles and refugees found paradise.

# Acknowledgments

Writing this book was helped immeasurably by the support of John Cerullo, Carol Flannery, Gail Siragusa, Liz Smith, Dale Olson, Marc Wanamaker, Marje Schuetze-Coburn, Claudia Gordon, and the still lively ghosts of Hollywood.

Billy Wilder (right) and Erich von Stroheim on the set of 1943's *Five Graves to Cairo*. Directed by Wilder (who also co-authored the script), the war film starred Franchot Tone, Anne Baxter, and von Stroheim as Field Marshal Erwin Rommel.

# Film Noir Goes Mainstream

## *The Genius of Billy Wilder*

Before the opening of *Sunset Boulevard* in 1950, Paramount showed it to many leaders of the movie industry in their largest screening room. Aside from screenwriters invited to the event who were delighted to be depicted as sexy leads in the film—Joe Gillis, the male lead, and his girlfriend are screenwriters—most of the audience, including Louis B. Mayer, then head of the industry's biggest and richest studio, was enraged.

As related by Maurice Zolotow in his biography of Billy Wilder, the film's director and co-writer, Mayer strode up to Wilder after the screening and shouted, "You bastard!" shaking his fist. "You have disgraced the industry that made you and fed you. You should be tarred and feathered and run out of Hollywood!" Then Wilder did something unthinkable in the studio-controlled Hollywood of the time. He looked the mogul in the eye, pulled his ever present homburg hat down tightly on his head, and spat back, "Fuck you!" According to witnesses, the silence was deafening as Mayer turned and walked away. What Wilder had done in his black tragedy, now recognized as the greatest movie about the movies, was to break a cardinal rule in Hollywood: he told the truth. Even in the entertainment capital of the world, fame and beauty are only temporary.

Not only were many in Hollywood angry with Wilder's perceived irreverence toward the film industry, they were also dismayed with the direction films were taking at the time. But change was hardly surprising. After a decade of war and economic upheaval, the light-hearted films that had been a Hollywood mainstay for so many years (musicals constituted a big part of MGM's fame) didn't seem, well, honest anymore. For many, in this post-depression, postwar world, movies were no longer relevant unless they reflected reality rather than presenting a fantasy.

Beginning in Germany in the late 1920s, such a new film style was emerging. In 1925's *Greed* and *The Wedding March* (1927), the famed Austrian director and actor Erich von Stroheim introduced elements drawn from German expressionism: cynicism, irony, eroticism, and dramatic cinematography were all part of the new filmmaker's manual. Far different from the old-world escapist sophistication found in the work of directors of the previous generation—F. S. Murnau and Ernst Lubitsch (an idol of Wilder's), much of the new style was drawn from the nihilistic response to the chaotic political and economic reality of the times, found especially in jazz-age Berlin, where many of the filmmakers honed their art.

Hallmarks of the new style also included the naturalistic precision of details in settings by means of camera technique (lots of oblique lines), dramatic cutting, and chiaroscuro lighting (dark shadows, aside from their emotional power, were one answer to financial constraints imposed by worldwide economic depression: they hide empty spaces on sets).

The film *M*, made by Fritz Lang in 1931, is an near-iconic example of the new style. In it, Lang succeeded in presenting a psychologically sound portrayal of a criminal, with scenes set against a realistic back-drop of Berlin-as-Düsseldorf. *M* was a far cry from a typical—or even great—American film of the era like that year's *Grand Hotel* or King Vidor's terminally sentimental *The Champ* (not to mention the typical American western): as different from the standard Hollywood product as a nightmare is from a daydream.

Like many refugees, when Wilder arrived in Hollywood during the Christmas season of 1934, he had few possessions and little money in his pockets. To survive, he lived wherever he could; among his homes was an anteroom outside the women's toilets in the basement of the Chateau Marmont Hotel. But he persisted, and in only a few years he would begin his rise to fame with 1941's *The Major and the Minor*.

Today many filmgoers remember him for creating such comic masterpieces as *The Seven Year Itch* and *Some Like It Hot*, but his impact on American—and world—film was much deeper. In 1943, through the marriage of his German expressionistic style with the tough-guy writing style of crime novelist Raymond Chandler (who also co-wrote the script), Wilder made the first great American film in the new style soon called film noir: *Double Indemnity*. Based on a hard-boiled shocker of a novel by James M. Cain and evoking a seedy world of bored, brutal, middle-class characters unredeemed by any virtue except cunning, *Double Indemnity* is, says one film expert, "the first film which played film noir for what it essentially was: small time, unredeemed, unromantic." Biographer Richard Armstrong particularly cites one scene in *Double Indemnity* (the dumping of Dietrichson's body at the railroad tracks) as a defining example of the new style. Shot night-for-night (the filmmaker's term for shooting nighttime scenes at night instead of in a darkened set) for maximum gloom, the scene's deep shadows, gritty streets, dramatically lit staircases, and barren desert-scapes were, in their powerful moodiness, pure noir.

It almost didn't happen. Like the later *Sunset Boulevard*, *Double Indemnity* came as a shock to the industry, but in this case was almost blocked by the combined efforts of Paramount, the Hays Office (the Hollywood censor), and the film's male star, Fred MacMurray. He hated the film. MacMurray's sense of propriety also crossed him up seven years later when, after Montgomery Clift turned down the Joe Gillis role in *Sunset Boulevard* (Clift considered the story too close to his June/December relationship with the aging torch singer Libby Holman), Wilder offered him the part. MacMurray excused himself because playing a "kept man" offended his moral values. Paramount then ordered contract player William Holden to take the part, and it

made him famous (Holden was nominated for an Oscar for his performance in *Sunset Boulevard*, but lost to Jose Ferrer. He won an Oscar
for 1952's Billy Wilder–directed *Stalag 17*, and was nominated again
for his performance in 1976's *Network,* which was won posthumously
by his co-star Peter Finch).

Nevertheless, *Double Indemnity* was made, released, and became
the archetype of the noir film style to which audiences responded
with enthusiasm; within three years, clones were flying off studio
production lines. In 1944, it would become the first clearly noir film
to be nominated for an Oscar (actually two nominations: Best Picture
and Best Actress for Barbara Stanwyck). Although there are many
of the stylistic elements of noir in *Casablanca*, the film that won the
Best Picture Oscar the previous year, most film experts consider it
too romantically conceived to be considered pure noir.

Besides the screenwriters, another person in the audience that
night in 1950 when Wilder screened *Sunset Boulevard* also loved the
film—or at least saw a great chance to stage a show for the press. After
the screening, Barbara Stanwyck approached the film's once legendary
star Gloria Swanson, who as the faded screen star Norma Desmond
was more or less playing a chapter out of her own life. Overcome by
the film and weeping, Stanwyck knelt down, crumpled the hem of
Swanson's silver-lamé gown in her hand, and kissed it.

*Sunset Boulevard* is, of course, much more than a star turn for a
once great star, although it surely is that. Much of the film's fascination lies with Wilder's uncanny juxtaposition of reality and illusion.
To play the role of Norma Desmond, a person who lives in the past,
Wilder first approached Mae West, who was outraged that she was
even considered for the role of a has-been actor seeking a comeback.
He then asked Pola Negri and Mary Pickford, both of whom were
equally horrified at the idea. Then he offered it to Swanson, who a
generation earlier had been the highest-paid actress in the world.
Ironically, the story of a fictional comeback attempt would be her
vehicle for a real comeback.

The line between fact and fiction doesn't stop there. Throughout Desmond's house in the film are many framed photographs meant to be images from the fictional star's past; in fact, they are all real pictures of Swanson from *her* past. In the movie, Desmond screens part of a silent film for the young reporter she falls in love with (Holden) to see; the film clip is actually from Swanson's 1928 movie *Queen Kelly*, made when she was being paid $250,000 a week (the equivalent of $2 or $3 million today). And playing the role of Desmond's butler in *Sunset Boulevard* was none other than the great director Erich von Stroheim, who directed *Queen Kelly*.

Billy Wilder may have been raised and trained with the concept of noir flowing in his blood, but he didn't invent it and never claimed he did. But for American film, by defining the noir canon in *Double Indemnity* and celebrating it in *Sunset Boulevard* he was certainly its leading Hollywood midwife.

His European point of view, filtered through what in retrospect we can only define as genius, also allowed him to create a dozen or so other films in entirely different genres with equal success. Among them were such enduring classics as 1954's *Sabrina,* 1955's rollicking romantic comedy *The Seven-Year Itch;* 1957's *Love in the Afternoon*, the courtroom drama *Witness for the Prosecution,* made the same year, and the comic farce *Some Like It Hot* in 1959. In 1945 he made *The Lost Weekend*, and in 1960 *The Apartment*, for which Wilder became one of only three people to ever win three (or more) Oscars for the same film: as producer (Best Film), screenwriter, and director. (The others were Charles Chaplin, who won a special award for acting, writing, directing, and producing *The Circus* in 1928, and Peter Jackson, who won producing, directing, and screenwriting Oscars in 2003 for *Lord of the Rings: Return of the King.*)

Sophisticated cynicism may have defined Wilder's persona to the world, but words, despite his discomfort with English which he always regarded as a foreign language, were his genius. In Wilder's first directing job in Hollywood, 1941's *The Major and the Minor*, the humorist and actor Robert Benchley would utter one of filmdom's most famous one-liners: "Why don't you get out of that wet coat and into a dry Martini?" After Benchley died in 1945, most of his obituaries credited him with the line. Wrong. It was, of course, Wilder's. Throughout the many films he wrote (basically with only two collaborators), Wilder's facility for words was celebrated. There is one exception. The most famous line in *Some Like It Hot*—Joe E. Brown's "Well, nobody's perfect" response when Jack Lemmon, in drag, tells Brown he's really a man after becoming "engaged" to him—was improvised on the spot by Brown.

Billy Wilder was born Samuel Wilder on June 22, 1906, in Sucha, a village in the then Austro-Hungarian province of Galicia that is now part of modern Poland. His mother, who had lived in New York for several years when she was a young girl, loved all things American, especially Buffalo Bill, on whom she once had a crush. As Wilder later confided to Ray Milland, star of *The Lost Weekend,* that's why she nicknamed him "Billie," and the name, albeit later spelled in a masculine manner, stuck. Billy first studied law, but soon began work-ing for a tabloid newspaper in Vienna. Seeds of his future cynicism were planted early. When Billy was a child, he saw the emperor Franz Josef in a parade. He was followed by his great grandnephew Otto von Hapsburg, clad imperially. Years later, as a refugee in the United States during World War II, Otto would ask Wilder for a job.

It was the American jazz bandleader Paul Whiteman, who was responsible for Billy's move to Berlin. Impressed with the interview Wilder did of him for a newspaper, he invited him to accompany the band to Berlin to write notices for what would be the first jazz concert ever given in a German-language country. Billy was instantly captivated by the Berliners' aggressiveness and brittle wit and soon got a job as a reporter (he became a close friend of Erich Maria Remarque, then a fashion-magazine editor, who would later write the great anti-war novel *All Quiet on the Western Front*). One day when Billy got the idea of doing a piece on gigolos for his paper, he hired himself out as one of the dance partners then supplied by the major hotels for unescorted women. A subsequent series of articles got him a job at the biggest Berlin newspaper and made him one of the most familiar faces in the city.

Yet he wanted a bigger audience; that could only be achieved through screenplays. And Berlin was, for a time, the perfect place to be, with hundreds of small studios. For the next few years Wilder would write and ghostwrite two hundred scripts; appropriate to his tabloid background, he received his first screen credit on *The Devil's Reporter* (1929). In 1933 he fled the mounting Nazism to Paris, and thence to Hollywood at Christmastime in 1934. The rest is movie history.

Of course, Wilder didn't do it all alone. In fact, during all his years in Hollywood he never wrote a script by himself (he always felt he needed an American-born writer to deal with the subtleties of the American vernacular).

His first Hollywood screenwriting collaboration was with the Harvard-educated novelist and drama critic Charles Brackett. It started in 1936 and lasted some fourteen years, probably setting a record for a writing partnership (they did, however, take a short vacation from each other when Wilder wrote *Double Indemnity* with the notoriously difficult, alcoholic, Raymond Chandler). And they didn't just write for Wilder's own films: among their credits was legendary director (and fellow exile) Ernst Lubitsch's *Bluebeard's Eighth Wife* (1938) and Howard Hawks's *Ball of Fire* (1941), a spinoff of one of their most famous collaborations (written with Walter Reisch), 1939's *Ninotchka*, Greta Garbo's celebrated comedy and next-to-last film.

It was, in fact, Wilder's anger over director Mitchell Leisen's changes in the script the pair wrote for *Hold Back the Dawn* in 1942 that caused him to plead with Paramount producers to allow him to direct a film. Confident that he would fall on his face and thus end the matter, they gave him the Ginger Rogers/Ray Milland starrer *The Major and the Minor*. When the film became a huge commercial hit, Wilder was, overnight, a director to contend with and went on to direct twenty-five more movies.

Billy's next long-term screenwriting partnership was with the Romanian-born Isadore Diamond, who, feeling that his name sounded too Jewish when he entered Columbia School of Journalism, adopted the three initials I.A.L.; nevertheless, everyone called him Izzy. This collaboration lasted a quarter century and spawned, among others, such classics as 1954's *Sabrina*, *Witness for the Prosecution* in 1957, *Some Like It Hot* in 1959, and 1960's *The Apartment*.

Wilder also had an uncanny ability to pull great performances from actors, even when, like Marilyn Monroe, they were impossibly difficult to deal with. In 1968, nine years after making *Some Like It Hot*, his second movie with Monroe (the first was 1955's *The Seven Year Itch*) and six years after her death, he recalled, according to Maurice Zolotow, in his book *Billy Wilder in Hollywood,* "It's getting to be an act of courage to say anything but saintly things about her. Well, let me be courageous. Marilyn was mean. Terribly mean. The meanest woman I have ever met around this town. I have never met anyone as utterly mean as Marilyn Monroe; she was the meanest woman I have ever met around this town . . . or as utterly fabulous on the screen."

Nevertheless, most people agree that her best films were the pair directed by Wilder. Although Monroe, as was her habit, was always late, bad-tempered, and unsure of her acting, which consisted mainly of batting her eyes, twisting her mouth, and wiggling her rear, Wilder managed to coax memorable performances out of her, syllable by syllable. "It was like pulling teeth," he later recalled. Shortly after completing *Some Like It Hot*, he observed, "You can take forty-two takes of her in one scene, and then you take her aside and say, to calm her down, 'Don't worry, Marilyn,' she'll look at you with wide-open eyes and say, 'Don't worry about what?'"

"She has breasts like granite, and a brain full of holes, like a Swiss cheese. She hasn't the vaguest conception of the time of day," he once said of working with her. "[When] she arrives late, [she] tells you she couldn't find the studio where she's been working for years." (On the first day of shooting *Some Like It Hot*, despite having a one o'clock call, Monroe showed up at three-thirty and emerged from her dressing room at six.) According to Wilder, she habitually blew even the simplest lines; after fifty-nine takes of the scene in which she couldn't manage "Where's the bourbon?" he had cards placed everywhere with the line written on them; even then, she blew it eight more times. Her co-stars found her equally frustrating. When asked what it was like kissing her, Tony Curtis snapped, "It's like kissing Adolf Hitler."

So how did Wilder handle her, coincidently turning her into one of the most celebrated stars in American film? With infinite patience. Never once during the production of *Some Like It Hot* did Wilder find fault or lose his temper with her, not even on the last day of shooting when she didn't show up at all after learning that the picture wasn't going to end with a scene featuring her. When her husband, playwright Arthur Miller, later sent a savage telegram to Wilder criticizing his comments about Monroe and blaming him for her miscarriage, Wilder replied that, rather than abusing her, he pampered her, despite her lack of consideration for her co-workers or the production schedule. "Had you, dear Arthur," he wired Miller back, "not been her husband but her writer and director, you would have thrown her out on her can. . . . I did the braver thing. I had a nervous breakdown."

*The Apartment* (1960) is still considered by many as the most sophisticated film ever made in Hollywood, although there has always been debate over how it should be classified. Once when asked how it should be described—as a drama, a comedy, or a love story—Wilder said, "It doesn't fit into any specific category. It's a film that is trying to say a few pertinent things about the society we live in in this year of Payola, 1960." (Payola was the then notorious synonym for bribery.) "We sugarcoated the story with a few laughs here and there," he said of the script. "But what we wanted to say in it finally was: human beings are human beings."

Although some of the (generally favorable) reviews considered the story about a man who lets his boss use his apartment for extramarital rendevous sordid, Wilder went on to score his Oscar hat trick. Sometime later, Shirley MacLaine, the female star of *The Apartment,* suggested the reasons had to do with his discipline, as well as his story ideas: "He can be as disciplined as a soldier and as soft as velvet. Billy Wilder has a complete blueprint for his film before he starts shooting. . . . His script is such a polished product that he knows exactly how it will work."

His next film, *One, Two, Three,* was another spoof of the American way of life. This time he poked fun at the attempts of a Coca-Cola representative to make his the national drink on the other side of the Iron Curtain. It was also received with mixed reviews, although the majority were enthusiastic. (In making it, James Cagney, the film's star, blew just about as many of his lines as Monroe blew in making *Some Like It Hot.*)

His next film, 1963's *Irma La Douce,* was based on the 1956 French musical; this rather noir comedy was seen by Wilder as another chance to challenge Hollywood's belief that a screen comedy should be composed only of sweetness and light. In adapting the musical, Wilder threw out everything but the name, determined to make a new kind of story about a Parisian streetwalker. Starring Shirley MacLaine, it would be sentimental and bittersweet, rather than a clichéd social document about a hard-boiled woman of the world. "It will strike a happy medium between Tennessee Williams and Walt Disney," Wilder told one visitor to his set. Indeed, as the *Los Angeles Times* wrote: "(Ernst) Lubitsch, who delighted in sex farces, stopped at the bedroom door. Wilder walks right inside." Other than a few negative reviews (among them one from the otherwise sophisticated *New Yorker* magazine), Wilder had another hit on his hands. "[Wilder's] gone and done it," raved the *New York Times.* "He's taken this little tale of a brash Parisian poule and her mec (pimp) and run it into a charmingly antic romantic comedy."

The next year saw *Kiss Me, Stupid,* a film that, by carrying the scandalous stories of *The Apartment* and *Irma La Douce* to a new level, got the filmmaker in trouble. Although the then powerful Catholic Legion of Decency considered the earlier films offensive to Christian and traditional standards of morality, they, nevertheless, awarded the films their qualified "B" rating. *Kiss Me, Stupid,* however, received the Legion's first condemned rating in the eight years since 1956's *Baby Doll,* and no wonder. The story is about a small-town songwriting team determined to break into the big time and a famous singer (played by Dean Martin) who can bring it about if the female member of the team slept with him. "(Wilder) has regrettably produced a thoroughly sordid piece of realism which is aesthetically as well as morally repulsive," was the opinion of Bishop Thomas Little, the Legion's executive secretary. Although the noir side of Wilder may have been gratified by the Legion's "sordid bit of realism" comment, he was stunned with the reviews that were almost unanimously bad. "Suddenly I was a celluloid Rasputin," he said. "What the critics call dirty in our pictures they call lusty in foreign films." And, indeed, *Kiss Me, Stupid* was far better received in Europe, where a British film magazine hailed it as the "punchiest American comedy since *The Apartment* . . . about thirty times as funny and memorable as the best of the Hollywood rut."

Wilder fled to Switzerland for a year to recover, and it would be many more months before he and Diamond could come up with an idea for another film. "We shall survive," he said. "We shall now come out with a Mustang (a reference to the fastest-selling car in the history of the Ford Motor Company, introduced in 1964) and sweep the market." It didn't quite work out that way. The film *The Fortune Cookie* (starring Walter Matthau and Jack Lemmon) did well enough—Matthau won the Oscar for Best Supporting Actor—but the response was nowhere near as ecstatic as that for his earlier films. Nor were his last films, including 1969's moody *The Private Life of Sherlock Holmes*, well received, and 1972's *Avanti*, despite starring Jack Lemmon and Juliet Miles, seems to have been Wilder's least successful film.

In 1950, Wilder made a classic noir film, *Ace in the Hole*, about an opportunistic reporter played by Kirk Douglas who, by exploiting the human-interest aspect of an accident, turns it into a tragedy. In 1974 he returned to the journalism theme with a remake of the 1931 hit play by Charles MacArthur and Ben Hecht, *The Front Page*. Starring Jack Lemmon and Walter Matthau, both too old for their parts, it brought, at least in the opinion of some critics, nothing new to the newsroom, particularly compared to Howard Hawks's unforgettable 1940 screwball comedy *His Girl Friday*, based on the same play and starring Cary Grant and Rosalind Russell.

Two years later Wilder tried a return to his greatest success. If *Fedora* wasn't his idea of a remake of *Sunset Boulevard*, it's mighty close to it . . . even to casting *Sunset Boulevard*'s leading man in the role of a down-at-the-heels movie producer playing opposite an aging star. Made with German tax-shelter money, it sat on the shelf for a year and a half. "Unlike violins and wine, pictures don't get better with age," Wilder said at the time when United Artists finally released the film in 1974, spending an insulting $625 on an advertising campaign. Nevertheless, the *New York Times*'s Vincent Canby called it "seasoned, elegant, funny and hugely entertaining," and the same paper's Janet Maslin wrote of it: "A fabulous relic . . . old-fashioned with a vengeance, a proud, passionate remembrance of the way movies used to be . . . Rich, majestic, very close to ridiculous, and also a little bit mad."

Wilder admitted the resemblance. "I made *Sunset Boulevard* thirty-one years ago," he said in 1981. "A painter is allowed to paint in the same style. Surely, one is allowed variations on a theme, some added thoughts. There's nothing I can do to change *Fedora* now," he added. "It's last year's snow. It's melted. It's gone."

In 1981 Wilder's last film, *Buddy, Buddy*, was released. Again starring Matthau and Lemmon, it was a prototype of the hit-man comedy now fairly popular.

Billy Wilder died in March 2002 at the age of ninety-five. He was survived by his wife of more than fifty years, Audrey, who years before appeared as the hat-check girl in *Lost Weekend* (only her arm handing Ray Milland his hat survived the cutting-room floor).

At the time of *The Fortune Cookie* disappointment, Wilder, uncharacteristically defensive, compared himself to a then notorious, foul-mouthed, anti-establishment comic. "So now maybe they still think I'm the Lenny Bruce of pictures. The jury has already found me guilty of vulgarity and no talent. But really, I see nothing wrong with myself. Perhaps obscenity, or vulgarity, is in the eye of the beholder."

So, too, was Billy Wilder's undoubted genius.

Screenwriter Salka Viertel hosted what was probably the most influential Hollywood salon of the 1930s, which gave many famous émigrés a place to gather, gossip, and recall their cultural roots.

# 2
·······

# The Catalyst

## *Salka Viertel*

"The ties that bind" is a phrase that has been used to define relationships ranging from religion to sports, a description of commonalities of interest that define most of us to ourselves and to others. So it is not surprising that when the thousands of German-speaking filmmakers, artists, writers, and intellectuals fled Europe in the 1930s and early 1940s because it was no longer safe to remain at home, the ties that bound many moved right along with the exodus.

For some, they bound nearly too tightly; many German-speaking refugees remained exactly that in their new Southern California home: German-speaking refugees. Aside from those working in the film industry, who had no choice, more than a few continued speaking German, refusing to learn English or even associate with their new neighbors. The great writer Thomas Mann was one who simply avoided contact with the natives for some time after his arrival in 1940. Alma Mahler Werfel was another.

Since many of the new arrivals knew one another in Europe before emigrating, their social and cultural traditions were as vital in Southern California as in, say, Berlin (although the *wurst* and beer weren't as good). And for the émigrés who worked in the film industry it was fairly easy to maintain those ties—they were in constant contact with one another, at the water cooler, in the studio canteen, and in the workplace. And many within the film industry, as well as non-industry émigrés, had another method to maintain the apartness they brought along with them—the salon.

Popular since, probably, Renaissance times, the salon provided a setting for thinkers and doers to meet, socialize, and discuss matters of current and esoteric interest. In New York during the 1920s, the salon to be invited to was the one hosted by Mabel Dodge at her Fifth Avenue home. It regularly attracted such guests as the late journalist Walter Lippman and the young Communist John Reed (with whom she had a torrid affair, well treated in the movie *Reds*. Dodge subsequently married Tony Luhan, a Pueblo Indian, and reigned as the social queen of Taos, New Mexico).

Most of these ties that bound the émigrés together were embodied in the unlikely life of a refugee writer and actor named Salka Viertel. For many of the émigrés who arrived with little beyond the tattered remains of their once-great European reputations, the salons Viertel hosted at her home at 164 Mabery Road in Santa Monica were much more than social gatherings. For such uprooted talents—especially for the many talented professionals who were forced to take menial jobs to survive in their newly adopted land—the gatherings were life rafts formed from a few cherished hours of speaking in their native tongues and commiserating with friends and compatriots about surviving in a somewhat alien paradise.

Among those friends were Bertolt Brecht and Thomas Mann's brother Heinrich. Neither, as we will see elsewhere in this book, were successful in Hollywood, despite having great contacts and credentials.

But the salon, at least in Hollywood, served a grander purpose, too. In a time when many things German were being discarded for the duration (much German music was dropped from symphonic programming, as well as the repertory of the Metropolitan Opera Company), such salons were a small but, considering the social environment, brave effort to protect a liberal vision of the German culture at the very moment it was being so gruesomely perverted on the world stage.

For years, Salka Viertel's 1969 autobiography *The Kindness of Strangers* (named for a line from Tennessee Williams's play *A Streetcar Named Desire*) has been considered a sort of time machine to visit the émigrée personalities of Hollywood's golden age. And not just the German émigrés; British novelist Christopher Isherwood, who fled his native England not because of persecution, but because he was a pacifist, lived near Viertel's Santa Monica Canyon home and, for a time, even rented her garage apartment. One visitor recalls looking into the Viertels' living room one afternoon and seeing the great pianist Arthur Rubinstein tinkling the piano keys while Bertolt Brecht was arguing politics with another visitor. And as Viertel made her living by writing screenplays (most notably co-writing Greta Garbo's *Queen Christina*) for MGM, her book has also been considered valuable for the historic and political insights into the once powerful studio system.

But it has become clear, both from reminiscences and recent research, that Viertel, like members of the film industry before and since, whitewashed the real story. Marta Feuchtwanger, wife of the celebrated German historian Lion Feuchtwanger and hostess of another famous salon for German-speaking émigrés in Los Angeles, once said she admired Viertel's book most for what Salka had *not* written. Out of, apparently, a strong feeling of discretion, Salka had refrained from mentioning just about all of the most interesting things, which according to Marta, would have made the book a sensation had she included them. Among those interesting things were many details about the ties that bound Salka and many of her group.

Although rarely discussed at the time because of box office concerns (nothing is sacred in Hollywood except protecting the box office), it was common knowledge within the industry at the time that Salka, along with Greta Garbo, Marlene Dietrich, and stars like Gloria Swanson, Janet Gaynor, and Barbara Stanwyck, were part of a huge underground lesbian—or at least bisexual—element in Hollywood society. Until the mid-twentieth century, when witch hunts like those led by Senator Joseph McCarthy and the U.S. House Un-American Activities Committee sent Hollywood running for cover, Hollywood's lesbian population was, like the film capital's huge gay population, an open secret, acknowledged and dealt with like any other power base or trade union. More than a few of Viertel's glamorous cast of characters were lesbians or, at least, swung in whatever direction was pleasurable or profitable. Only in 2000, with the publication of journalist Diana McClellan's meticulously researched book *The Girls*, was this reality of Hollywood's golden age of filmmaking revealed to a new generation.

As an example of this sort of 1930s double-think, consider Cary Grant. Two decades ago, in the light of his multiple marriages and testimony by Dyan Cannon, his fourth wife and mother of his only child, the common wisdom held that the actor was heterosexual despite rumors based on his longtime friendship with fellow actor Randolph Scott.

Yet for many years after 1932, when the twenty-eight-year-old British acrobat named Archie Leach—soon to adopt the screen name of Cary Grant—came to Hollywood (after a stay in Manhattan where he roomed with a gay Australian named Jack Kelly, later to become famous in Hollywood as the movie fashion designer Orry-Kelly), his "gayness" was hardly a secret. It was also openly discussed and supported by direct testimony from such friends as director George Cukor, George Burns, and Grant's later secretary Frank Horn. Jimmy Fiedler, a powerful radio gossip columnist of the time, once sniped of Grant's very public friendship with Scott: "These guys are carrying the buddy business a bit too far." And actress Carole Lombard was once quoted in the *Los Angeles Times* as saying, "I wonder which of those guys pays the bills?" Grant himself more or less admitted it years later, albeit obliquely: "I pretended to be somebody I wanted to be," he once said. "And finally I became that person."

Salka's Viertel's husband, Berthold, a poet by nature but a film and stage director by necessity, is treated more like a ghost moving through *The Kindness of Strangers* than the tormented person and husband he was. Some have suggested that his relative failure in Hollywood was because, in both his professional and private lives, he was locked into the German expressionism cult of the 1920s even after it had long fallen out of fashion (you could say the same thing of Brecht, but although he complained, unlike Berthold Viertel, he managed to survive on what he could eake out in the film capital).

Because of his self-perceived genius, Berthold felt entitled to withdraw from the responsibility for material things, turning the covering of living expenses, the education of their sons, and the cost of the house (which Salka bought with his permission for $7,500 after the 1933 Long Beach earthquake temporarily depressed the Los Angeles housing market) over to Salka. This was excused by their friends, who included the director (and fellow émigré) Fred Zinnemann, Christopher Isherwood, and Salka's onetime lover Gottfried Reinhardt (son of Max), as a writer's prerogative (although most successful writers, including the Viertels' friend Thomas Mann, are usually highly disciplined).

Perhaps a sense of unreality is all right for a writer, but Berthold was forced to make his living as a director, and for a director, particularly one working in the film industry, to be successful, it is imperative to be organized. Reinhardt once commented: "The activity and the authority connected to it [making films] open outlets for preoccupations or concerns which either have nothing to do with stage and film, or do so only on the periphery—such as politics, sociology, psychiatry, historical revision, and playing with style." In other words, ignore the basic responsibilities of film and stage direction, and you risk losing the public. This wasn't a new problem with Berthold. His first wife, Grete, was cynical about his unsuccessful attempts at a film career. She once commented that Berthold, an infallible genius in his own mind, had one weakness: silk shirts. As silk shirts were expensive, only working in the highly remunerative film industry would make them possible.

At least Viertel treated her three children, Hans (John, born in 1919), Peter (born in 1920), and Thomas (born in 1925), more three-dimensionally in her book. After publishing his novel *The Ely Story* in 1950, John, who had worked with Brecht in Santa Monica, as well as at the Reinhardt Studio in Berlin before the family moved to California, decided on an academic career on the East Coast, where his close friend the famous linguist Noam Chomsky lived. Chomsky's friendship with Brecht later led to his participation in the 1989 documentary *My Name Is Bertolt Brecht—Exile in USA*.

Salka, who worried over Thomas's future when he was a sickly child, needn't have . . . he did just fine. After studying at UCLA, he went to work for the city of Los Angeles (first in municipal administration and then as a social worker, which better suited his sense of justice and for values in life) and wrote poetry. Thomas Viertel is the only one of the sons who remained in Los Angeles.

Peter Viertel followed in his mother's writing footsteps; his greatest fame rests on having been chosen by director John Huston to doctor the final version of the script for Huston's film *The African Queen,* and on his 1953 book based on that experience, *White Hunter, Black Heart* (with a screenplay by Viertel, it was made into a film in 1990, produced and directed by and starring Clint Eastwood). In 1960 he married actress Deborah Kerr; until recently the couple lived in Klosters, Switzerland, where, because of their presence, Salka spent the last years of her life. In 2001 Peter appeared in the television special *Greta Garbo: A Lone Star*, hosted by Lauren Bacall.

Peter is said to have been the model for the character played by Robert Redford in the 1973 social comedy *The Way We Were,* and the character played by Redford's co-star Barbra Streisand is based on Virginia Ray Schulberg, nicknamed "Jigee," who divorced the novelist and screenwriter Budd Schulberg (*What Makes Sammy Run?*) to become Peter Viertel's first wife in 1942.

For years Greta Garbo (left), then the most famous actress in the world, and Salka Viertel had an intimate relationship that benefited the careers of both. In the 1933 remake of Garbo's first talkie, *Anna Christie*, in German, Salka was cast as the waterfront whore Marty (right).

Certainly whitewashed in Salka's book, however, was the true story of the relationship that was central to her career for a decade and to her life for forty years: her intimate friendship with Greta Garbo. The most famous actress in the world in the 1930s (as well as the most unapproachable), Garbo was Salka's calling card to Hollywood, as well as her clout in getting what she wanted: recognition, money, and companionship. Everyone in the industry knew that to get to Garbo—certainly to get Garbo to make a film—the best way was to go through her friend and, apparently, occasional lover Salka Viertel. So it isn't surprising that Salka was hired by MGM as a screenwriter, although her primary responsibility was to suggest ideas for movies acceptable to the difficult star when she was at the height of her fame (Viertel's secondary trump card was her knowledge of Central European literature and drama, which she could draw on for possible film subjects). And it paid off—in fact, of the last ten films Garbo made, five were for MGM: 1933's *Queen Christina*, 1934's *The Painted Veil*, 1935's *Anna Karenina*, 1937's *Conquest,* and the last, *Two-Faced Woman,* in 1941.

When the need for Garbo ended, so did Salka's career. That happened when *Two-Faced Woman* flopped at the box office after opening on New Year's Eve in 1941. But the failure of the movie—and the subsequent ending of Garbo's career—wasn't just because *Two-Faced Woman* was a bad film (although it was). The European market, the source of the best earnings for Garbo films, had more or less evaporated, thanks to the war. So if Hollywood no longer needed Garbo, Hollywood no longer needed Salka Viertel; in some ways, the loss of Viertel was a blessing in disguise for the film industry since, with her departure, the studios no longer had to put up with her outspoken (leftist) politics.

Salka Viertel was born Salomea Steuermann on June 15, 1889, in the small town of Sambor, then in the Austro-Hungarian province of Galicia, now Poland (not far, incidently, from the place where Billy

Wilder, who would co-write Garbo's 1939 hit *Ninotchka*, was born seventeen years later). She was the oldest of four children born to Josef Steuermann, a lawyer and mayor of the town, who once aspired to be an opera singer.

They lived outside the town in a large rambling house named "Wychylowka," Polish for "leaning out." For the rest of her life, Salka would herself lean out of her way to re-create the warm ambiance of Wychylowka, which boasted a river, a dense forest, and an orchard with hundreds of fruit trees. There was enough money for the children to have German and French governesses, and all the Steuermann children spoke both languages—in addition to their native Polish—fluently.

Salka was no beauty, but, nevertheless, still an attractive, appealing, redheaded child. In her maturity in Hollywood, she radiated the charm and culture of old Europe, one reason for her success with the German-speaking émigrés. (Another, according to the refugee director Fred Zinnemann, was her love of gossip.) Her Galician-formed hospitality was expressed in almost unbelievable generosity—which at times could go to extremes of recklessness and extravagance—and in her joy as an excellent cook serving her guests old dishes of *Mittel*-Europe, including Apfelstrudel, Gugelhupf, and other fattening pastries.

From early childhood she wanted to be an actress. It was first expressed when, at the age of four, Salka built a small stage in the corner of her room and filled it with characters cut from fashion magazines. Her improvised plays would run for days, with Salka speaking all the parts before an audience of her siblings and household servants. Her fascination with the theater grew, and when she was fifteen and a friend of the family suggested she move to Vienna, she loved the idea and eventually made the move.

It wasn't long before she encountered another young actor whom she also whitewashed from her memoirs. In Vienna, one of her first roles was that of an Amazon in a production of Heinrich Kleist's *Penthesilea*; another of the Amazons was played by the teenaged Marlene Dietrich, and when Dietrich succeeded to the lead in the play, Salka became her understudy. Nevertheless, in *The Kindness of Strangers*, other than for an oblique reference to "Mary" Dietrich, the famous actress and singer is a nonperson. Why? Perhaps it was because Garbo and Dietrich (and Salka), off and on, later shared the same lover . . . the American poet, playwright, and lover-to-the-stars Mercedes de Acosta (whom Salka, incidently, introduced to Garbo). Garbo, despite having made at least one film with Dietrich, also claimed never to have met the lady. Perhaps Salka promised Garbo never to mention Dietrich's name, but couldn't resist putting something in her book for the cognoscenti. Garbo, as was well known at the time, enforced all sorts of privacy rules on her friends—if you violated them, she never spoke to you again.

Salka also lived in Berlin for a time, sharing an apartment with her brother Edward, who was a musical apostle of Arnold Schoenberg, who was then just beginning to arouse controversy over his twelve-tone music composition theories. Years later Schoenberg and his wife would become regulars at Viertel's Santa Monica salons, and on a visit in 1936, Edward, a pianist, appeared as a soloist with Otto Klemperer and the Los Angeles Philharmonic at the Hollywood Bowl.

In 1916 Salka was introduced to Berthold Viertel, then on leave in Vienna from the eastern front, who immediately announced that he would divorce his wife and marry Salka. It would have to wait until the completion of his military obligation, but on April 30, 1918, the couple was married in the city's Seitenstaeder synagogue. The early months of the marriage were difficult, marred by separations caused by their careers, which ended when, because of civil disturbances in the city, Salka was released from an acting contract in Munich. She then joined Berthold in Dresden, where he had been appointed director of the Royal Saxonian Theater.

Following the birth of Hans, they moved to Berlin, where Salka continued her acting career, occasionally directed by Berthold. There, and later in Düsseldorf, they were thrust into a social milieu that, before anyone suspected, would be resurrected in the living room of a house in far-off Santa Monica, California. Bertolt Brecht was one of their friends; so was the operetta star Fritzi Massary (who would, like Brecht, come to Hollywood as a refugee and become part of their circle). Another member of their crowd was a young Communist named Otto Katz, who many years later and going by the name of André Simon, would be executed by the Stalinists in Czechoslovakia, where he was minister of state; unknown to many then and now, he was the first husband of Marlene Dietrich, and this fact, along with the virtual erasure of Dietrich from *The Kindness of Strangers*, is another of Salka's curious omissions from her book. Perhaps it was motivated by the Dietrich issue; more likely it was because Salka's own leftist leanings had often gotten her into trouble. The fact remains that Katz/Simon would not only be a frequent guest at the Mabery Road salons, but he was also a buddy of Berthold Viertel when he stayed in New York during his separations from Salka.

While coping with a rapidly enlarging family, and finances at "their lowest ebb," thanks partly to Germany's out-of-control inflation, salvation for the couple arrived from a hardly imagined source. Fox offered Berthold a three-year contract, engineered by the famous director F. W. Murnau, to write and direct films for the studio (when told, Salka's reply was said to have been "Where is Hollywood?"). After stopping off in New York for several weeks, Salka and Berthold arrived on the Santa Fe Chief amid the orange blossoms of Pasadena's station in 1931.

Among the first to welcome the couple to their new home with a large party at their Hollywood Boulevard mansion were Emil Jannings and his wife (Jannings, who co-starred with Marlene Dietrich in *The Blue Angel*, would not stay a friend long. Soon he would be back in Germany, hailed as a national treasure, and blaming the Jews for bringing on their own problems). Other guests included the legendary director of sophisticated comedies, Ernst Lubitsch, and actor Conrad Veidt. First renting a small house on Fairfax Avenue near Hollywood

High School (". . . the least expensive house I could find," recalled Salka in her memoirs), the family soon moved to the Mabery Road house near the beach in Santa Monica Canyon; their rent was $900 for three months, lowered to $150 a month when their stay was made permanent. They also bought a Buick (which Berthold, who could never tell the difference between the accelerator and the brake pedal, promptly damaged), hired a housekeeper, and began entertaining old friends from Germany.

Among their first guests were Albert Einstein and his wife; he was then considering an offer to join the California Institute of Technology in Pasadena before he finally chose Princeton. And within weeks of their arrival, the couple met Greta Garbo, who was enjoying the enormous success of her first "talkie," *Anna Christie* (the theater marquees famously proclaimed: "Garbo talks!"), at a black-tie party given by the Lubitschs. Salka, who spent the evening drinking champagne with the star on a secluded veranda, was, like most who met Garbo, awestruck. "Books have been written about Garbo's beauty, mystery, and talent," Viertel recalled. "There is something unexpected in the loveliness of this face. She was intelligent, completely without pose, with a great sense of humor."

The next day as the Viertels finished their lunch, "the doorbell rang, and in the open window . . . appeared the unforgettable face," Salka wrote. "In the bright daylight she was even more beautiful. Gaily she announced that she had come to continue the conversation of last night, and stayed all afternoon. We went for a short walk on the beach, and then sat in my room. She lived not far from us and in the evening Berthold and I walked her home. (Thereafter) she came very often early in the morning when the beach was deserted, and we took long walks together.

"[One day] Garbo asked me: 'Why don't you write?'"

Thus began the relationship that would change Salka's life and career, and eventually end Garbo's.

Initially, Salka resisted the change, claiming that she was not a writer but an actress. In fact, she would be working with Garbo as an actress when, in 1933, MGM remade *Anna Christie* in German and Salka was cast as the waterfront whore Marty, played by the older character actress Marie Dressler in the first version of the movie. While making the film, Salka came across a biography of Queen Christina of Sweden, whose life had been the subject of a play written by the country's national playwright August Strindberg.

Garbo loved Salka's suggestion that she play the part of the lonely queen and urged Salka to write a script. The timing couldn't have been better; Garbo's contract with MGM was expiring, and the studio was "moving heaven and earth to make her sign a new one," Salka recalled. Garbo showed the proposed screenplay to MGM's production boss Irving Thalberg; he agreed to make the film; Garbo signed a new contract; Salka was hired to co-write the new screenplay; and after the usual dramatic showdowns between the principals, *Queen Christina* was made. Directed by Rouben Mamoulian, it would be one of Garbo's most unforgettable roles, culminating in an iconic closeup of the famous face as her ship sails. Her love interest in the film was played by John Gilbert, Garbo's ex-lover and co-star from 1927's *Flesh and the Devil* (Gilbert, his career virtually ended when sound came in 1928, was cast on Garbo's recommendation after the studio decided the original choice for the part, Laurence Olivier, didn't have the acting ability needed).

But it was her character's interest in her lady-in-waiting (played by Elizabeth Young), culminating in a passionate screen kiss, that gave the film much of its notoriety. And, of course, unsuspected at the time was how accurately the story of a queen who remains unmarried and eventually abdicates her throne would parallel Garbo's own career.

"I have repressed memories of *The Painted Veil*," Salka writes of the film that she co-wrote for Garbo after *Queen Christina. The Painted Veil*, based on a novel by W. Somerset Maugham and set in China, was poorly received (as one critic said, the best thing about the film was Garbo's costumes in this rare—for her at the time—modern-dress film). It was followed by the far better *Anna Karenina,* produced by David Selznick and based on Leo Tolstoy's novel. Salka Viertel co-wrote the screenplay.

Salka didn't, however, work on Garbo's next film, MGM's lavishly produced *Camille* (1936), one of Garbo's greatest films. Again, Viertel whitewashes history. In fact, you have to search Viertel's book closely to find any mention of the movie. Perhaps one reason was that, at the time, Salka was obsessed with making a movie based on the life of Marie Waleska, Napoleon's mistress, with Charles Boyer as the emperor. Made the following year as *Conquest,* it was generally well received, but reportedly lost more money for the studio than any film made from 1920 until 1949. It also signaled the end of Garbo's costume dramas.

Garbo's next film was one of her best, and again Salka had nothing to do with it. In fact, she had decided (admittedly with Garbo's permission) that the actress would be perfect to portray Madame Curie, the woman who won the Nobel Prize for the discovery of radium in 1898. She even went on a studio-financed trip to Europe to explore the project with Curie's heirs, and a treatment was written by the famous novelist Aldous Huxley. "It was instantly forgotten," Viertel says (Curie's life was made into a film in 1943, starring Greer Garson, with Huxley as an uncredited screenwriter). The reason for MGM's disinterest? They decided that Garbo's image was getting too dour and decided to lighten it with a comedy. The one they chose, her only full-length comedy, was a triumph for the actress: *Ninotchka.*

Playing off the success of the "Garbo Talks!" tagline of *Anna Christie* a decade earlier, *Ninotchka* was marketed as the film in which "Garbo Laughs!" The idea was so good that the creator of the story, Melchior Lengyel, was able to sell it to the studio based on a three-line description: "Russian girl saturated with Bolshevist ideals goes to fearful, Capitalistic, monopolistic Paris. She meets romance and has an uproarious good time. Capitalism not so bad after all." The title was chosen from the name of Garbo's character, a Russian envoy sent to Paris to expedite the sale of some jewels.

Billy Wilder and his partner were brought in to polish the script, and the great Ernst Lubitsch was hired to direct. Cary Grant was the first choice to play opposite Garbo as her Parisian paramour Count Leon d'Algout, but when he turned down the part, the role went to dashing Melvyn Douglas, who had starred with Garbo once before in *As You Desire Me* (1932). It was a delicate matter to actively criticize the politics of the Soviet Union and Communism in 1939, but *Ninotchka* pulls it off with its use of satire to demonstrate the draw of Western culture and capitalism (nevertheless, when released, it was banned in the Soviet Union). Garbo's role as a woman in a position of power—a serious, intelligent, and dedicated party member—was also bold for its time.

In the meantime, Salka had been fired by MGM after her newly hired agent made salary demands it considered unfair, but was rehired when she came up with an idea they thought would be a surefire follow-up to the success of *Ninotchka*. The film, *Two Faced Woman*, was a failure and spelled the end of Salka's association with the studio (although she would write several more screenplays in Hollywood). It was, as it turned out, the end of Garbo's fabled career as well.

It has often been said that Garbo chose to retire from cinema after this film's failure, but, in fact, she simply became more choosy about her roles. The years passed; projects were offered and died stillborn; and she faded into a very high-profile retirement in New York, where until her death in 1990, one of the most popular avocations of her neighbors was "Garbo-spotting."

A problem for Salka was the evolution of the screenwriter's job, which by and large now demanded an author who could write and deliver a polished script complete with dialogue, and not just a film subject or treatment. Salka, who loved California, was, nevertheless, drawn back to Europe by circumstances after she had nothing left in

America. She was no longer sought after as a screenwriter. Berthold had remarried an actress, Elisabeth (Liesl) Neumann, and died in 1953. Her sons had moved on, and she had given up the Mabery Road house for a smaller one on Carmelina in Brentwood. And, of course, Garbo was gone.

So she moved to Klosters, Switzerland, where her son Peter also settled; at the time the small mountain village was very popular with the "beautiful people." She invited Greta Garbo to visit in the early 1960s, and she did, renting a home near Salka's. As Viertel grew older, she would often order her dinner sent in by the Hotel Pardenn; so did Garbo, but instead of ringing the doorbell and placing the dinner on the dining room table as at Salka's, the hotel employee would ring Garbo's bell but leave the meal outside. One other of Salka's frequent visitors was Berthold's widow, Liesl, and it is said that Garbo used to laugh when each greeted the other with "Good-day, Mrs. Viertel."

In July 1969 Salka returned to Los Angeles, but her arthritis prevented her from doing much socializing with the few friends like Marta Feuchtwanger who still remained. She soon returned to Klosters.

Her old friend and tenant Christopher Isherwood visited Salka in Klosters in 1972 with his lover Don Bachardy, and returned for a second visit five years later, about the time she had become so ill that she needed a full-time nurse (Viertel then also hired a friend to look after Garbo when she was in town).

Salka Viertel died on October 20, 1978, at the age of eighty-nine, and is buried in Klosters's Protestant cemetery. Greta Garbo visited the grave annually until 1988, when she was no longer able to travel from New York.

Fritz Lang examining a film negative. Note monocle, for which the imperious Austrian émigré was famous, in his left eye.

# 3
·······

# The Monocled Aristocrat

## *Fritz Lang*

It may be true that Frank Zinnemann and Billy Wilder became the most successful of the refugee directors in Hollywood, but in the beginning of their careers, the most famous was Fritz Lang. When he arrived in Hollywood in 1934, he was probably the most famous of all German filmmakers and was generally treated with awe by all and sundry. There is no question that the most important contribution made by the fifteen hundred or so German-speaking refugees and émigrés working in the film industry—film noir—had its roots in the pioneering work, as well as the pessimistic viewpoint, of this aristocratic, Viennese-born talent, considered by many one of the undisputed geniuses of the silent-film era.

Friedrich Christian Anton Lang was born in Vienna on December 5, 1890, and thus grew up during the last days of the Austro-Hungarian Empire's fin de siecle, an artistic and intellectual heritage he carried with him all his days.

His father was a fairly well-to-do architect and later construction executive; his mother was a Jew, who, in accordance with the Catholic Church's law concerning marriage to non-Catholics, had agreed that her son would be raised a Catholic. His godfather was Christian Cabos, a purveyor to the Austro-Hungarian Imperial Court. In 1908, after initially studying civil engineering, he switched to art, reveling in the sensuality of such Viennese artists of the time as Gustav Klimt (who would also influence the young Alma Mahler).

During 1910 and 1911, he traveled extensively in Africa, Asia, and the Pacific, selling drawings, painted postcards, and cartoons to support himself, eventually settling in Paris. In July 1914 he left Paris when anti-German sentiment rose after the murder of Jean Jaures, a then famous (or infamous, depending on your politics) Socialist who had worked toward French–German amity as tensions rose between the countries. They would explode in World War I; Lang was drafted, assigned to the Russian front, and received several citations for bravery. After being wounded four times (once with a shrapnel splinter in an eye) and suffering from shell shock, he was declared unfit for military service and released with the rank of lieutenant in May 1918. After convalescing for a year in a Vienna hospital (during which he began writing screenplays), Lang moved to Berlin and joined the UFA studio.

Although film noir came to its maturity in America in the 1940s and '50s, when Berlin's mid-war cynicism was married to the new hard-boiled style of the American novel in a low-budget environment demanded by depression-era economics, the early and among the most successful examples were created by Lang while he was at UFA. The 1931 *M*, Germany's first sound film, which starred Peter Lorre as a compulsive child-murderer, is today acknowledged as an early masterpiece of the genre (it was also Lang's favorite of his films, but not the first reflecting Lang's dark vision).

In fact, throughout his work, certainly starting with his early film, 1921's *The Tired Death* (*Der meude Tod*), one is confronted with Lang's fascination for using film to explore, as he himself admitted, "cruelty, fear, horror, and death," from which, he demonstrated, a flowering of truth can bloom. His was a preoccupation with the dark side of human nature: vengeance, violence, and the criminal mind.

Recently released on DVD as *Destiny*, the film was also Lang's first hit. Echoing the demonic side of German folklore, the story line allowed Lang to fill the screen with exciting spectacle, as well as to create a truly unique character (Death), whose influence can be found in Ingmar Bergman's symbol-filled *The Seventh Seal*, made thirty-seven years later. The story: after a young man is abducted by Death on his honeymoon, his bride is allowed to beg for his return. Death yields to her entreaties and agrees to deliver back the life of her husband if she can find someone who would give up his life in exchange. The bride's efforts to find a sacrifice follow as she visits three exotic locales (Persia, Venice, and China); in each she fails to find someone to fulfill the bargain. In a dramatic ending, she then takes the only step she can to reunite herself with her lover. Lang's point is that while love cannot overcome death, it retains a power that even death would respect and envy.

*Destiny,* heavily influential in its own time, has remained so. We've spoken of its influence on Bergman; it was also the film that first sparked interest in moviemaking for Luis Buñuel, the father of cinematic surrealism. Its influence can also be found in, among others, Roger Corman's *Masque of the Red Death* (1964), Mario Bava's *Lisa and the Devil* (1976), and Terry Gilliam's 1985 masterpiece *Brazil.* As unlikely as it seems, and probably for its depiction of exotic locations, the film is also claimed to have been the original inspiration for Douglas Fairbanks, Sr.,'s 1924 feature *The Thief of Baghdad.*

Lang followed *Destiny* with *Dr. Mabuse, Der Spieler* (1922), a two-part portrait of a master criminal, and then made 1924's five-hour epic *Die Niebelungen* (released in the United States in two parts, *Siegfried* and *Kriemhild's Revenge*). Based on the thirteenth-century Siegfried epic (the primary myth that inspired Richard Wagner's four-opera cycle *The Ring of the Nibelung*), Lang intended it to restore pride in Germany's cultural heritage. He achieved far more.

*Die Niebelungen,* in fact, has been called the "grandaddy of all fantasy epics" and "German silent cinema at its zenith." More recently, it has been hailed as the silent film equivalent of Peter Jackson's *Lord of the Rings* trilogy. Dealing with deeds of valor and codes of honor and filled with dwarves, magic, blood oaths, ferocious battles, the film is seemingly far removed from Lang's signature style. But what Lang is really doing is exploring the results when those honor codes are carried too far, and the devastating consequences of raw emotions. The parallels to what would happen in Nazi Germany a few years later are truly startling. Lang, one observer has said, showed the world what would happen twenty years before it did.

And to many he also showed what else was wrong with the modern world in what is, after *M*, Lang's most celebrated film—1926's *Metropolis*. Written by his second wife Thea von Harbou, who provided the scenarios for most of his German films, *Metropolis* is a powerful— if somewhat simplistic—expressionistic drama about a futuristic slave society in which the powerful live in skyscraper gardens high above the proletariat, who live in a subterranean world.

A year and a half in its making, *Metropolis* was the filmmaker's attempt to top his German epics and directly challenge Hollywood's entertainment primacy, a result, in part, of the First World War (the influence of Eisenstein's *Battleship Potemkin* can also be seen—it opened in Berlin just as *Metropolis* was going into production). Eisenstein was, in fact, photographed with Lang and the *Metropolis* crew, as were many celebrities of the era—in 1925 Berlin it was a sign of being part of the smart set to have been allowed to watch Lang and his wife at work (Billy Wilder, then a screenwriter in Berlin, and Hitchcock also visited the set).

Costing ten times more than the average Hollywood film of the era, the film bankrupted UFA, the famous German film consortium that financed it which had to be reorganized and recapitalized (primarily with money from Paramount and MGM), forcing Lang to form his own production company to make his next film, *Spione* (*Spies,* 1928). It was followed in 1929 by *Woman in the Moon* and then in 1931 by *M*.

Nevertheless, even when it was made, *Metropolis* was recognized as the most ambitious picture since D. W. Griffith's epic *Intolerance* of exactly a decade earlier (which bankrupted Griffith's company). Three-quarters of a century before computers made it possible to create fake crowds and, indeed, the sets themselves (as in *Gladiator* and the later *Star Wars* films), Lang ingeniously used mirrors to place thousands of extras in the same frame as his vast miniature sets, designed in a pretentious Art Deco style that could be described as "Mussolini-Moderne." Like *Destiny, Metropolis* has had its influence on later filmmaking (including James Whale's 1931 *Frankenstein, Blade Runner*, the *Batman* series, even *Flash Gordon*).

It has also been written that no movie more aggressively marketed the Marxist message of social relations, with its visual metaphor of an urban proletariat buried under the city it built. The critic Roger Ebert has hailed *Metropolis* as doing what great films can do . . . by creating a time, place, and characters so memorable that they become part of our cultural images for imagining the world.

If *Metropolis* was planned to, in part, challenge Hollywood, what Lang did with *M* began a sea change that would one day actually change Hollywood. Consider: when *M* was made in 1931, it was as far from the typical—or even great—American film of the era as a nightmare is from a daydream. That year MGM's *Grand Hotel* was hot box office on Main Street U.S.A., as was King Vidor's *The Champ* (not to mention the typical American western). But *M*, a realistic portrayal of a criminal in the social milieu of Weimar Republic Berlin, dealt with reality as Lang saw it.

"If Adolf Hitler had never existed," the critic Andrew Sarris has written, "Fritz Lang would have had to invent him on the screen." Lang followed *M* with 1933's *Das Testament des Dr. Mabuse* (*The Last Will of Dr. Mabuse*), in which he used a madman in an asylum as a spokesman for Nazi doctrines.

After it opened, the filmmaker was summoned by Joseph Goebbels, Hitler's propaganda minister, and the story of that meeting is the most famous anecdote of Lang's German career, and one that may, in part, be apocryphal. Goebbels reportedly told Lang that *Dr. Mabuse* was being banned in the Reich as "an incitement to public disorder." Nevertheless, he was so impressed by Lang's ability that he invited him to supervise German film production. Unknown to Goebbels, Lang was planning to leave Germany anyway, and because the meeting with

Hitler's propaganda director ran so long, the banks were closed when it ended, and Lang fled to Paris leaving behind a personal fortune and a vast collection of primitive art.

We know Goebbels told Lang of the ban on his film . . . that much is recorded in Goebbels's appointment book. But we also know that Lang left Germany with most of his money and, unlike most refugees, and made several return trips later in the same year. One reason for his departure was probably his utter opposition to film censorship, which he saw would be a problem in Germany. In fact, years earlier he had spoken on the subject in a way that still resonates: "[I do not believe] a people to whom the state had documented its belief in its political maturity by giving it the right to vote needs a guardian just because some claim it is not mature enough to know what might be good or bad for it. I have nothing against the state introducing restrictions for youths; it's fine with me, but it should not dictate for adults the kind of relaxation, regeneration and fortification their nerves need."

Another reason for his departure might have been his suspicion that, although he was not Jewish, his mother converted from Judaism to Catholicism a decade after his birth, which would have made his heritage highly equivocal had he remained in Germany.

In 1933 Thea von Harbou divorced Lang and enthusiastically joined the Nazi movement. Lang, incidently, was a notorious womanizer who enjoyed the romantic company of Kay Francis, Marlene Dietrich, and Joan Bennett. He had countless other affairs, drove at least one rejected starlet to suicide, and was dogged throughout his life with the story that he murdered his first wife, Lisa Rosenthal. In 1920 she was found dead in the couple's apartment, shot with Lang's pistol. The rumor was that Rosenthal shot herself after finding Fritz and von Harbou—whom he would marry soon after Rosenthal's death—in a state of undress. A darker story held that Lang may have pulled the trigger himself, although there is no proof.

He knew how to use women for professional, as well as sexual, advantages. In the late 1920s, von Harbou so relentlessly championed

Lang's career that the famed writer Dorothy Parker once remarked of Lang: "There's a man who got where he is by the sweat of his frau."

After making one film in France in 1934 (*Liliom*, starring Charles Boyer), Lang signed a one-picture contract with David O. Selznick of Metro-Goldwyn-Mayer and moved to Hollywood. Received by the German-speaking community as more or less a deity, Lang would remain in the film capital for the next twenty-one years (he became a citizen in 1939), making twenty-one films in such various genres as thrillers, war and crime dramas, and westerns.

Despite such films as 1937's *You Only Live Once* (based on Schiller's story of a man driven to criminal behavior through lost honor), Lang never succeeded in translating his European eminence to Hollywood. His personality was the problem. Despite his reputation as Germany's greatest director, his elitist posturing infuriated many co-workers—for some years the tall, physically imposing Lang continued to use a monocle and affected a Continental formality. To many of the émigrés and refugees, as well as the native-born Americans in Hollywood, his demeanor resembled that of the imperious Prussian side of the enemy, an image ironically derived in part from Lang's own anti-Nazi films *Man Hunt* (1941) and *Ministry of Fear* (1943). If this alone wasn't enough to set teeth on edge amid the informality of Hollywood, his temperamental nature and dictatorial behavior on movie sets did. His German accent grated on the actors to whom he barked commands, and he refused to compromise with his idea of perfection—a crippling defect when dealing with the studios.

He developed a strong interest and love for the mythology of the American West, living for weeks at a time on Indian reservations. He also became fascinated with American slang. His Hollywood debut, *Fury* (1936), a study of mob violence starring Spencer Tracy and Sylvia Sidney, was a huge commercial and critical success. It was followed by *You Only Live Once* (1937); *You and Me* (1938); two westerns for the 20th Century-Fox studio, *The Return of Frank James* (1940) and *Western Union* (1941); and a series of war films, thrillers, and melodramas, including *Hangmen Also Die* (1943), which Lang wrote in collaboration with Bertolt Brecht. These were followed by 1944's *The Ministry of Fear* and *The Woman in the Window* (1944) and the following year's *Scarlet Street* (one of the saddest of the film noir genre and Lang's favorite among his Hollywood films), both starring Edward G. Robinson. The later films, mostly crime dramas, included Clifford Odets's *Clash By Night* and *Rancho Notorious*, a western made in 1952 and famously starring Marlene Dietrich; *The Big Heat* (considered by many his best Hollywood film) and *The Blue Gardenia* (1953); *Human Desire* (1954); *Moonfleet* (1955), a costume drama; *Beyond a Reasonable Doubt* and *While the City Sleeps* (1956).

After 1944's *The Woman in the Window*, Lang failed to have any more commercial successes, and despite having eight more films greenlighted, it was all downhill from there. Not even the fact that his salary was a relatively modest $50,000 per picture (Hitchcock was then getting $250,000) could save him in an industry where his personality had already alienated many. He even began falling out with his compatriots; the friendship between him and Bertolt Brecht—both shared a disgust of California-style consumer capitalism—ended with their contentious collaboration on *Hangmen Must Die.*

He left Hollywood to direct two low-budget films in India and in 1959 returned to Germany, where he completed his career circle by directing his final film, *The Thousand Eyes of Dr. Mabuse*, in 1960 as he was becoming increasingly blind. In 1963 he portrayed himself in the film *Mopris,* an act of homage by Jean-Luc Godard released in the United States as *Contempt.* Lang was awarded the French Officier d'Art et des Lettres for his body of work.

In the mid-1960s Fritz Lang returned to America, where he stayed actively interested in politics, fulminating against the new governor of California, Ronald Reagan.

He died in Beverly Hills, California, on August 2, 1976, at the age of eighty-five.

At the turn of the century Alma Schindler was considered the most beautiful girl in Vienna; by the time she arrived in Los Angeles in 1940 after fleeing Nazism in a months-long walk across Europe, she looked "like a bag of potatoes." Nevertheless, throughout her life, she inspired many of the era's greatest creative talents, marrying the composer Gustav Mahler, the revolutionary architect Walter Gropius, and the poet/playwright Franz Werfel before imperiously dominating Hollywood's German émigré society.

# 4

• • • • • • •

# The "Muse to Genius"

## *Alma Mahler*

A lthough the matronly sixty-one-year-old woman would probably never admit it (she was much too convinced of her self-importance for that), her arrival in Los Angeles on December 30, 1940, with her playwright/novelist/poet husband in tow, was far less important than another event that day. For on this penultimate afternoon of America's last full year of peace before war engulfed the world, the Pasadena Freeway—then called the Arroyo Seco Freeway because of its location in a dry riverbed—was opened after years of planning and construction. It would set a pattern for rapid transportation in America that would be both praised and cursed.

The arrival of Alma Werfel, wife of the writer Franz Werfel, widow of the once famously controversial Austrian composer Gustav Mahler, and former wife of Walter Gropius, architect-founder of the Bauhaus, was merely the latest of a flood of German-speaking refugees fleeing Adolf Hitler's Fortress Europa. And like the Pasadena Freeway, she would be praised and cursed.

Once considered "the most beautiful girl in Vienna," by the time of her arrival in Los Angeles, she, according to one writer, looked "like a bag of potatoes" in her signature black dress and fake pearls. Despite the fact that her new home provided the first haven from war she and her husband had known in nearly a year, she disliked Los Angeles, often likening her time there to that of Roman nobility residing in the back provinces. In this she was hardly alone. Like many fellow

Germans and Austrians, she rarely spoke any language but German and rarely dealt with the local populace, preferring to socialize with fellow émigrés. Nevertheless, for a decade, as she did in pre-Nazi Austria and to a lesser extent in New York, where she lived for the last twelve years of her life, Alma would reign over a mini-kingdom of sycophants, admirers, and fellow refugees that included the Nobel Prize–winning writer Thomas Mann and his family, the conductor Bruno Walter (who started his career as Gustav Mahler's assistant), the Austrian refugee composer Erich Korngold, and others sharing similar roots.

Like the German exiles drawn to the salon hosted by screenwriter Salka Viertel in Santa Monica, fellow refugees and émigrés were drawn to her gatherings for the opportunity to keep alive the German cultural traditions amid the chaos of total war. Many were attracted to her by the dramatic saga of her flight from Nazi Europe. For Thomas Mann, her appeal had a lot to do with the sort of attention she devoted to the people she respected. "She gives me partridges to eat, and I like them," he said. But Alma Mahler Werfel's main claim to fame was the men she had slept with. No one liked the fact that, despite having two Jewish husbands (and a number of Jewish lovers), she was—and remained all her life—a notorious anti-Semite.

Gustav Mahler, then as now, was the most famous and among the first of her celebrated liaisons. It was as his wife that the young Alma first encountered America a generation before her arrival in Hollywood, and it was not a happy experience.

A 1910 issue of New York's *Musical Courier* explained what happened to end the Mahlers' three-year stay in Manhattan, where the composer/conductor had previously led the Metropolitan Opera during two still legendary seasons. "It was a silly thing to bring a supreme judge like Mahler from Europe and place him under the direction of a petticoat jury" was the magazine's opinion of the troubles Mahler encountered during a short and highly controversial leadership of the New York Philharmonic Orchestra. Although the women of the Philharmonic's board were exasperated with the composer's imperiousness and his unpopular programming of new music (as well as a deficit of $75,000), Mahler was unhappy with the arrangement as well. "You cannot imagine what Mr. Mahler has suffered," Alma, told the press at the time. "In Vienna (where he previously led the Imperial Court Opera) he was all-powerful. Even the emperor did not dictate to him, but in New York he had ten ladies ordering him around like a puppet." The following year the Mahlers returned to Europe because of the composer's swiftly deteriorating health; he would die of a blood infection in a sanatorium in Neuilly, France, on March 11, 1911; his last written words were scrawled across the manuscript of his unfinished Tenth Symphony. "To live for you, to die for you, Almschi." Today those ten ladies are long forgotten, and Mahler's music, the thing that was most important to him, is among the most popular in the classical repertoire, and that largely due to the support Alma, who in later years would describe herself as a "muse to genius," gave him. Actually, she was more than a muse where Mahler was concerned . . . she not only defended him with the tenacity of a guard dog, she also inspired several of his most immortal compositions, among them the lyrical Adagietto of his Fifth Symphony, composed in 1901 and dedicated to Alma the year before the couple married (the Adagietto was used memorably by director Luchino Visconti in his film *Death in Venice*).

The inspiration and strength that Alma gave Mahler and the other men in her life was discovered by her at an early age. And it was that strength that allowed her, well into middle age, to more or less single-handedly engineer a near-miraculous escape for herself and her husband Franz Werfel from Hitler's Fortress Europa, bringing along on their flight Heinrich Mann (the brother of the writer Thomas Mann, who was already living in the Pacific Palisades suburb of Los Angeles), Heinrich's wife Nelle, and Thomas Mann's son Golo.

Despite Alma's effort to piggyback her image on Gustav Mahler's fame for the fifty-three years that she outlived the composer, it was, in fact, her part in the epic escape from Naziism—and epic is the only word that describes it—that first defined her to the Hollywood exiles.

"They told us of the terror of their last days in France," Bruno Walter wrote in his memoir *Theme and Variations*, ". . . of the adventures of their flight, of Lourdes, where Werfel had been deeply impressed by the wonderful existence of the child Bernadette, or roamings that took them into the Pyrenees and finally of a night-bound mountain tour over goat paths up to the Spanish border and across it, Alma carrying the manuscript of Mahler's Third Symphony under her arm." Walter was wrong in the last regard. It wasn't the Mahler manuscript she was bringing out of Europe, it was that of Anton Bruckner's Third Symphony. The near priceless score, then being sought by Adolf Hitler, one of the greatest fans of Bruckner's music, was originally packed in her trunk, which disappeared for weeks during the couple's flight across Europe before reappearing inexplicably while she was in the south of France. Ironically, the symphony was the music played in the background when in May 1945 Berlin radio broadcast the news of Hitler's death.

The walk to freedom began on March 13, 1938. After withdrawing all her money in hundred-schilling notes from her Vienna bank and sewing it into a servant's and her own skirts, Alma and her daughter Anna (then, at thirty-four, a successful sculptor) boarded the train for Prague. It was the first leg of a flight to join up with Werfel in Milan, which became a seemingly endless and exhausting hegira as they crisscrossed Western Europe, walking for miles and relying for the most part on the kindness of strangers. (Anna eventually ended up in London, where she would sit out the war and help organize—with Sigmund Freud's daughter Anna—what seems to be the world's first children's day-care center, originally for orphaned victims of the blitz.)

During their flight they spent several weeks in the pilgrimage city of Lourdes in southwest France, a stay in Saint Bernadette's hometown that would have a profound impact on Alma and Franz's future. The little group eventually made it to Spain by walking over a pass in the Pyrenees and bribing their way through the border station with cigarettes and money. Within weeks they made it to Lisbon, where they boarded the Greek vessel *Nea Hellas*, the last regularly scheduled ship to sail from Lisbon to New York. When the group arrived in Hoboken, New Jersey, on October 13—seven months after Alma left Vienna—they were welcomed by dozens of friends, acquaintances, and the merely curious, who until they learned of the group's arrival in the newspapers, had presumed that they were dead. After spending a few weeks in Manhattan, where Werfel gave several lectures and Alma nostalgically revisited the landmarks of her stay with Mahler more than a generation earlier, they left for Los Angeles.

The couple was met at Pasadena's Santa Fe Station (LA's iconic art deco station wouldn't open for another year) by a circle of fellow émigrés who previously had settled under the palms, and were immediately escorted to the new home that had been rented for them—even the kitchen was fully stocked; so, too, was the bar, especially with the liqueur Benedictine, a bottle of which Alma would drink, sip by sip, every day for the rest of her life. Their friends had even hired a butler for the couple, who, Alma was delighted to find, was a former operetta tenor named August Hess. He would quickly become invaluable to the couple through his extreme reticence and devotion to Werfel's well-being. Hess was also a purebred Aryan, which added much to his appeal for Alma.

The couple's house, at 6800 Los Tilos Road, was perfect. An example of the ubiquitous red-tile-roofed Spanish-colonial Hollywood style of the 1920s and '30s, it hung (and still hangs) from a precipitous hillside hundreds of feet above the Hollywood Bowl. One enters directly into the living room where Alma and Franz swiftly gathered informal afternoon and evening salons; regulars included the novelist Lion Feuchtwanger and his wife Marta, Thomas and Katia Mann, the conductor Bruno Walter and his daughter Lotte, and many less solvent emigrants who had to work for a living, including Bertolt Brecht and Alma and Franz's fellow refugee Heinrich Mann, who for the rest of his life would scramble for a living as a screenwriter.

To take their minds off the exploding war (many émigrés would be glued to their radios after midnight when war news came through from London), most of the Werfel's guests would play games after dinner. The most popular was a form of charades that they called "The Game," in which half the group would pantomime a line of poetry or a famous quotation. Guessing the answer was always accompanied by loud shouts and hysterical laughter.

Down a narrow, wrought-iron spiral staircase in the house (called the "chicken ladder" by Alma, who by the end of the day and her bottle of Benedictine, often fell down it) were two bedrooms, plus an almost monastic room that Werfel used for a study. According to Susanne Keegan in her biography *Bride of the Wind: The Life of Alma Mahler,* it was there in a "tiny, whitewashed cell, just big enough for a narrow bed, a dresser, a table, and two chairs, that Franz, assisted by his secretary, Albrecht Joseph, wrote *The Song of Bernadette.* He started the novel within a week of the couple's arrival in Hollywood and finished it in five months. A year later it would be picked as a first choice by the Book of the Month Club and was quickly made into the film that would garner twelve Oscar nominations and win four, including the Best Actress Oscar for its star, Jennifer Jones, appearing in her first major role as Bernadette Soubirous. Again confirming the truism that the only thing that counts in Hollywood is the box office, appearing as the Virgin Mary in the film, a celebration of the Catholic faith if ever there was one, was Linda Darnell, who would in 1947 star in *Forever Amber,* famously banned by the Catholic Church. How Franz Werfel, a Jew, could write such an emotionally galvanizing novel about a Catholic saint was the subject of much controversy at the time. Werfel himself tried to explain it simply: he said that the great mysteries of divinity, redemption, and spiritual growth were to him (as they were, interestingly, to Alma's other Jewish husband, Gustav Mahler) part of a universal truth that reached far beyond any church's theology. His writing, he said, would ". . . magnify the divine mystery and the holiness of man . . . the ultimate values of our mortal lot."

He also felt the book was appropriate to those war-torn times. "None of my books, not even *The Forty Days of Musa Dagh* (a novel about the bloody 1915 battle between the Turks and Armenians), is so full of meaning," he wrote explaining the genesis of *Bernadette* in May 1942. "No one understands this war who still believes that it is a war of nations. Not a material but a spiritual principle is at stake. On one side stands radical nihilism that no longer regards the human being as the image of God but as an amoral machine. On the other side, our side, stands the metaphysical, the religious concept of life, the conviction that the cosmos was created by the spirit and that a spiritual meaning lives and breathes in every atom." Many, of course, still believe, as did Werfel, that World War II was a true contest between good and evil; certainly the movie audiences of the time did.

Alma Schindler was born August 31, 1879, in Vienna, the daughter of Jacob Emil Schindler, then the most famous Austrian landscape painter, and his wife, the former Anna von Bergen, who gave up a career as an opera singer when she married. When Alma was two, a sister, Grete, arrived, who was, after her mental impairment was discovered years later, institutionalized. In 1940 Grete was put to death as an "undesirable" by the Nazis, a family tragedy to which Alma characteristically reacted with indifference. When Alma was five, her father moved the family into a castle-like house, complete with a turret, in Plankenberg near the Vienna Woods. Her memories of the place remained so magical that, for all of her life, Alma would often recall scenes from her youth at Plankenberg as if they had just occurred. Equally magical to any child was the fact that, since neither parent believed in formal education, neither Alma (nor her sister) had to bother with schooling for years other than that provided by a tutor and their parents.

The idyll ended in 1892 when Alma's father died suddenly on a North Sea island vacation, but her adoration of him never stopped; after the city of Vienna erected a statue of him not far from those of Schubert, Mozart, and Johann Strauss, Jr., she would, for the rest of her life, send postcards of the statue to friends commenting how accurately the memorial captured his personality. She also became devoted to the piano and discovered a lifelong passion for the operas of Richard Wagner. At the age of fifteen she was finally sent to school, ostensibly to learn household arts for an eventual marriage, but such domestic interests were alien to a young lady already gaining a reputation for her looks. There is no evidence that Max Burkhard, director of Vienna's Burgtheater, was romantically involved with Alma, but there is no question of his impact on her life. Under his mentoring influence, she developed a love of the theater, a devotion to the writings of the philosopher Frederick Nietzsche and the poetry of Rainer Maria Rilke; for her sixteenth Christmas, he sent two servants carrying laundry baskets full of books for Alma, most of them leather-bound rare editions. There is also no question that her next relationship was physical and emotional, as well as intellectual. Gustav Klimt, then thirty-five, was a founding member and president of Vienna's secessionist movement, a group of artists organized to break away from the conservative traditions of the city's Imperial Academy. Alma's mother, who by now had married Carl Moll, a successful businessman (and later a high-profile Nazi), was determined to end her daughter's relationship with the bohemian Klimt. Despite Alma's claim that her mother's interference left her "on the brink of suicide" and the artist's declarations of "eternal" love, Alma soon fell in love with another. Today the composer Alexander von Zemlinsky is remembered more for being the mentor of the far more famous composer Arnold Schoenberg (who would also one day flee Germany for Los Angeles), but in his time he was famous in his own right. He was also, as Alma wrote after meeting the twenty-eight-year-old musician, "dreadfully ugly," but so, too, in the opinion of many contemporaries, was the far more important composer/conductor Gustav Mahler, whom she would later marry. Appearance meant little to Alma, who used the word "erotic" to describe a man's outstanding creative talent instead of his appearance or behavior ("unerotic" was her term for a man of no interest at all). For some women power is the ultimate aphrodisiac; for Alma it was communicating with those she considered cultural supermen. In short order Alma became a composition student of Zemlinsky and would go on to compose several attractive art songs. Given her beauty, as well as proclivities, it was inevitable that an emotional relationship would develop between them, the ultimate intimacy avoided only when Alma met at a dinner party on November 3, 1901 (also attended by Burkhard and Klimt), the diminutive (five-foot, five-inch) forty-one-year-old Gustav Mahler. Despite her claim that he made no impression (she refused his offer to walk her home to her parents' mansion), it wasn't long before a serious romance sprang up between the couple. "Mahler's image is alive in me!" she wrote a fortnight after the dinner and two days after hearing him conduct his First Symphony (which she "thoroughly disliked"). Her fascination with Mahler wasn't surprising. As director of Vienna's showcase Court Opera, a position reached via a fairly swift traversal of the then musical-directorship ladder, he was easily the most important musician in this music-obsessed city. He was "the jewel in Vienna's musical crown," according to one biographer. Born the son of an innkeeper and liquor merchant in Bohemia (now part of the Czech Republic), Mahler always felt he was a political outsider ("I am thrice without a country," he said, "a Bohemian among Austrians, an Austrian among Germans, and a Jew among all the peoples of the world"). He was also a musical outsider—at least as far as his own deeply subjective compositions were concerned. "I was composing before I could play scales," he once recalled, although there is little question that his prowess on the piano, which he started playing when he was four, was phenomenal.

In 1897 Mahler had converted to Catholicism, a move calculated to make him more acceptable as director of the Opera in anti-Semitic Vienna (Leonard Bernstein, a famous interpreter of Mahler's music, claimed much of Mahler's later music reflected an enduring guilt over his conversion). Such guilt as Bernstein suggests probably never occurred to Mahler, who had been raised in a home of freethinkers; had it, surely Alma Schindler, raised in Vienna's anti-Semitic environment, might have been less enthusiastic about him. One can't be sure, though; she once said of her husband Franz Werfel that "he could never write pure German because he was a Jew"; nevertheless, she unflaggingly championed his career and tenderly cared for him throughout a thirty-year marriage.

Mahler's notorious womanizing was just fine with Alma. "I was acquainted . . . with the scandals about him and every young woman who aspired to sing in opera," she once wrote. Mahler proposed to Alma within a month of the dinner party, and despite an appallingly insensitive letter the composer sent her demanding that if they married, she would have to forsake her love of composing music, the couple was married in a Catholic ceremony on March 9, 1902. By then, Alma was several weeks pregnant, and their first daughter, Marina, was born following a long and difficult breech delivery on November 3, one year to the date from that fateful dinner party. The couple was ecstatic over their baby Marina.

Marina, however, would die of scarlet fever in 1907, a tragedy that coincided with the diagnosis of Mahler's heart disease and his impulsive resignation from the Vienna Opera, all reflected in his darkest work, the Sixth Symphony. By then, however, another daughter, named Anna (after Alma's mother), had been born. For most of her life, she would have an uneasy relationship with her mother.

Anna and her mother were first estranged when Alma began a relationship with the architect and designer Walter Gropius while still married to Mahler. It was during a spa vacation in the summer of 1910 that Alma met the young, handsome, talented, and comfortably non-Jewish Walter Gropius. She was instantly attracted to him, and he to her; apparently they consummated their passion on the boat train from Paris to Cherbourg, where she was to embark with Mahler for what would turn out to be his final season in New York. (Gropius later founded the famed Bauhaus in Dessau, which from 1919 until 1933 was Germany's most important and most avant-garde art and design school.) There are some who attribute Mahler's early death to his heartbreak over the affair, but his frail constitution, along with the ongoing frustration over his New York problems, certainly contributed to his death.

Enter Oskar Kokoschka. When he was introduced to Alma by her father-in-law, the twenty-six-year-old Kokoschka was one of the most controversial poets and painters of his time; Klimt called him the "greatest talent of the younger generation." Archduke Ferdinand (who would make history by his death in Sarajevo three years later) wanted to "break every bone in his body" because of the eroticism of his paintings. One critic called the wrestling match between the light and dark, the passions and the spirit, in his paintings "Gauguin gone mad."

Both Alma and Oskar claimed the other had fallen in love at first sight. In any event, their affair was torrid: the "enfant terrible" and the seven-years-older "muse to genius." During a three-year relationship, Kokoschka painted two double portraits of himself and Alma, one clothed, the other naked, romping in a pastel Garden of Eden. Alma finally agreed to accept his endless proposals of marriage if he would paint a true masterpiece. He did (the painting, *The Bride of the Wind*, hangs in Basle, Switzerland). But, true to form, Alma, despite being pregnant with his child, was wearied by the intensity of the relationship and ended it. (Alma later claimed that her subsequent abortion released her from emotional bondage, although it devastated Kokoschka).

Eventually she took up the threads of her old life, which then meant the ever faithful Walter Gropius. The couple was clandestinely married in Berlin on August 18, 1915, when he was on leave from the 9th

Hussars, fighting in France. Despite the birth of a daughter, Manon, born October 5, 1916, the marriage was doomed. Alma believed it was Gropius's messianic vision of his Bauhaus movement, designed to unite architecture, sculpture and painting, and technology as a sort of religion for the masses, that—esoteric as it was—apparently cooled her ardor. She, as more than one observer has commented, liked her artistic nourishment less abstract and more immediate. Besides, by the fall of 1917, while Gropius was still at the front and two years before his Bauhaus became a reality in Weimar, she met another man—Franz Werfel.

Unlike Kokoschka's darkly sexual poems and art, Werfel's were lyrical affirmations of the human spirit, a positive side of the existential movement, which resonated so deeply with Alma that she had earlier set one of his poems to music (she had discovered the poem in a magazine bought from a book peddler's cart). She was instantly fascinated by his talent, as well as by his love for Mahler's music, and, despite frequent visits by Gropius, became pregnant by Werfel with her fourth child, Martin, born August 2, 1917. Gropius thought Martin was his child for some time. Sadly, Martin was sickly, suffered from brain damage, and died the following May. Gropius and Alma were divorced on October 20, 1920, after having harmoniously settled their differences over their daughter Manon's future.

Alma's daughter Anna said years later that the latter part of the 1930s, which ended with her mother's dangerous flight from Europe, were Alma's toughest years; she was, after all, married to a Jew in Nazi Germany. Far worse, however, was an event that occurred on April 22, 1935; Manon, Alma's beloved daughter, died at eighteen from polio. It was, significantly, Manon, who had grown up in the shadow of her mother's egocentricity, who comforted her mother. According to Karen Monson in her biography *Alma Mahler, Muse to Genius,* on her deathbed she said to Alma, "Let me die . . . you'll get over it, Mummy, as you get over everything." Then, possibly realizing her tactlessness, she corrected her farewell. "I mean . . . as everyone gets over everything."

It wasn't only Alma and Manon's father, Walter Gropius, who were crushed by her death. So was their friend the composer Alban Berg, who had received a commission for a violin concerto but was unsure of the form it should take. "Mutzi's [as Manon was known to friends and family] death provided the answer," he said: it would be "a symphonic poem with the character of a Requiem" dedicated "To the Memory of an Angel." (Soon after completing the concerto—today one of his most popular—in July 1935, Berg himself died of a blood infection.)

Franz Werfel's health, like Mahler's, was fragile, and the warning signs became apparent soon after the couple settled in Los Angeles. After the success of *Bernadette,* the couple moved to a more comfortable house in Beverly Hills, where since he was freed from the day-to-day details of living by Alma's management, Franz devoted himself completely to writing, including his new play *Jacobowsky and the Colonel* (to be directed in New York by the his fellow refugee Max Reinhard) and a novel, *The Star of the Unborn.* On September 12, 1943, after the couple and their friends had celebrated the completion of *Jacobowsky,* Franz suffered a serious heart attack followed by another three days later. Alma was terrified, but not for Franz . . . she thought death was a communicable disease and for that reason would never put a picture of a dead person next to one of someone living. Franz survived, but barely. In November he suffered another seizure while being x-rayed in the hospital, followed by another on December 14. On the following Thursday, December 23, the film version of *The Song of Bernadette* premiered, but Werfel was too ill to attend.

He recovered enough to return to his writing, completing *The Star of the Unborn* in August of the following year. On August 25 the couple dined with Bruno Walter and his daughter, and Franz danced a jig during a happy, gossip-filled evening. (Bruno Walter, Mahler's assistant years earlier in Vienna, bought the house next door to the

Bedford Drive residence in Beverly Hills to which the Werfels had moved a few months earlier.) The next day, after spending the morning lounging in the sun, Alma found Werfel dead beside his desk.

Despite the fact that her husband was a Jew, Alma demanded that the eulogy (which she wrote) be delivered by a Franciscan priest. Mourners included the Schoenbergs, the conductor Otto Klemperer and his wife, Thomas and Heinrich Mann and their wives, and Igor Stravinsky and his wife. While Bruno Walter played and replayed a Schubert sonata, mourners waited for more than an hour while Alma rewrote and rewrote the eulogy. Finally the service proceeded, but without Alma, who was driven the following day to visit her husband's grave in Hollywood's Rosedale Cemetery.

After Werfel's death and her move back to New York eight years later, the balance of Alma's life was somewhat of an anticlimax. In June 1946 she became a U.S. citizen. In 1947 she visited Vienna and was distressed to find that about the only friend left alive was Alban Berg's widow, Helene, who, suffering from dementia, didn't remember her. Alma's and her relatives' homes had been either destroyed or damaged, and her possessions had disappeared.

With the waxing interest in Mahler's music, she was being recognized more frequently as the years passed, but as Mahler's widow rather than Werfel's . . . and that didn't displease her. For her sixty-ninth birthday in 1948, opera and film composer Erich Korngold gave her a copy of his violin concerto, which he dedicated to her.

In 1952 she sold the Beverly Hills house and bought two apartments in a building on East Seventy-third Street in New York City. In it, two rooms were dedicated to represent what she thought were the major influences in her life; one room, known as The Power of Words, was filled floor to ceiling with her library. The other, which also served as her bedroom, was dubbed The Power of Music, and in it, along with several paintings by her father, was a Blüthner piano on which was a photograph of Gustav Mahler. For the next few years she was occasionally seen at major performances of her first husband's music. In 1962

Oskar Kokoschka asked to see her, but she refused him; apparently she didn't want the passion of her youth to see her as an old woman. Afterward he sent her a cable: "Dear Alma," it read. "In my [painting] *The Bride of the Wind* in Basle we are eternally united."

Alma Schindler Mahler Gropius Werfel's funeral was held at 5:00 P.M. on the cold Sunday of December 13, 1964, at Manhattan's Frank E. Campbell Funeral Home. Unlike the funerals of Judy Garland, held at Campbell's five years later, and Rudolph Valentino, sent on his trip to eternity in 1926 from Campbell's previous location, there were few visitors. Certainly no one stood in line to pay homage to the memory of the eighty-five-year-old woman in a tuber-rose-banked casket below the framed drawing of her as a child by her artist-father. Yet for a generation, particularly in Los Angeles in the 1940s, she and her husband Franz Werfel became an anchor for the dispossessed German-speaking refugees and exiles.

People have said that, despite her great bravery and imagination when she lead the escape from Nazi Germany, Alma lived her life in a dream world, seemingly untouched by some of the most tumultuous events in Western history, from the fall of old empires through tumultuous wars through the excitement and tragedy of John F. Kennedy. Was she a true "muse to genius," as she believed? Or was she the embodiment of the stereotype of the Hollywood star—superficial and silly?

Shortly before her death, Alma told her daughter that she was, in fact, back amid the bucolic joys of Plankenberg. She added that she had met Crown Prince Rudolf of Austria (forever romanticized in several *Mayerling* films relating the double suicide of Emperor Franz Joseph's son and his lover Maria Vetsera) on a mountain, and he wanted to have a child with her.

Alfred Hitchcock dictates changes in the script of his 1942 film *Saboteur* to his wife, Alma.

# 5

# The Master of Mystery

## *Alfred Hitchcock*

In *I Claudius* and *Claudius the God*, Robert Graves's epic novels of the Roman Empire, we join his protagonist on one occasion when the emperor is thinking about the best way to preserve his memoirs of his life and reign for future generations. Maybe they should be sealed up in a wall, he muses, or given to a priesthood to keep. Finally he decides that probably the best way for his memoirs to survive the centuries is just to leave them lying around somewhere.

Such, in some weird way, seems to be the heritage of the great film director Alfred Hitchcock today, twenty-six years after his death. Just about everyone—film fans, anyway—knows many of his films . . . certainly the great quartet made in the 1950s: *Rear Window, Vertigo, Psycho,* and *North by Northwest.* Equally celebrated by many are other thrillers from this master of the macabre: *The Birds, Marnie, Strangers on a Train.* But in the generation since his death in Los Angeles, to which he emigrated in 1939, many have forgotten how ubiquitous his very presence was. After he inaugurated his television series *Alfred Hitchcock Presents* in 1955 (with its successor, *The Alfred Hitchcock Hour,* there would be 267 episodes broadcast), other than for Cecil B. DeMille, he became the most familiar film director in the world. Part of the reason was his trademark cameo appearances in his films, a habit begun in the 1930s. Aside from DeMille, he was the only Hollywood director whose name attached to a film meant more at the box office than any of the stars in the movie.

But with the television series in which each episode was introduced and closed by him with slightly ghoulish humor, his recognizability reached—perhaps exceeded—such universally popular television stars of the era as Lucille Ball and Milton Berle. (Many people of a certain age can still hear in their mind's eye his ominously pitched opening: "Good eve-n-ing, ladies and gentlemen, and welcome to darkest Hollywood" is one example.) In fact, John Russell Taylor, who wrote the only authorized biography of Hitchcock, suggests that at his height, he was probably the most universally recognizable person in the world. Taylor adds that when a friend put this notion to "Hitch" (as colleagues called him), the director claimed it was nonsense until the friend challenged him to come up with an alternative. He couldn't . . . context was the problem. Film stars were (and still are) largely closeted; imagine Barbra Streisand (circa 1955) at your neighborhood delicatessen, or Robert Redford, when he was riding high from his *Downhill Racer* fame, on the No. 14 bus. Politicians, also, were often not recognized outside their own countries, Hitchcock's friend postulated; would anyone recognize Mao Tse-tung walking down the street in San Francisco's Chinatown? But Alfred Hitchcock would immediately have been recognized *as himself* in *any* context almost anywhere in the world.

No longer. But, like Claudius's memoirs left lying about, lacking his ubiquitous presence on the tube, as Hitchcock's physical image fades in our collective consciousness, the work he has left behind continues to burnish his image as one of the greatest and most unique filmmakers in the history of the medium. Maybe the reason is, as Taylor further suggests, Hitchcock is not only in his films, he *is* his films . . . and maybe that is what resonates so loudly these days when individuality counts for less and less. And that is the heart of Hitchcock's uniqueness, a film style designed to show how an ordinary man (or woman), alone and frightened, can overcome his anxieties by turning the tables on his enemies, forcing them—at least temporarily—into exactly the same vulnerable position.

A frequently told anecdote from his childhood supports this thesis. It seems that Hitchcock got into some mischief when he was five years old, and to teach him a lesson, his father sent him to the police station with a note asking them to put him in a cell. They did so for a few moments, after which the policeman released the child and told him: "This is what we do to naughty boys." The young Hitchcock was almost certainly scared out of his wits; combined with his rigorous Roman Catholic upbringing, the experience became a blueprint for future Hitchcock plots: terror inflicted upon the unknowing and sometimes innocent victim, often by the police pursuing an innocent person for something he or she didn't do; guilt, both real and apparent (simply being pursued by authorities is enough to convince many people of guilt); and, of course, revenge.

Alfred Joseph Hitchcock was born on August 13, 1899, in London, England, to William Hitchcock, a poultry dealer and fruit importer, and his wife Emma. He was their third child (his older brother, William, Jr., was born in 1890, and his sister, Nellie, arrived in 1892). The family—as was the custom of the time—lived above the greengrocer's shop. As noted previously, his parents were devout Catholics and brought their children up accordingly.

Like many children, as a child Hitchcock was fascinated with trains (also buses) and used them to travel all over London as a young boy. He was also particularly adept at memorizing public transportation schedules; some film writers have attributed the later methodical planning of his films to this trait. Train schedules are not improvised, nor were his shooting schedules when he became a film director.

As early as sixteen, when he was working as an illustrator, Hitchcock developed another fascination with the rapidly evolving art of film-making. In 1920 he was hired as a (silent film) title designer by the recently arrived branch of Hollywood's Famous Players-Lasky (which evolved into Paramount Pictures). He did this for two years when, finally, his entreaties to direct a film were heard. The movie, *No. 13*, was never finished when Famous Players-Lasky gave up the studio, but fate stepped in when an actor/producer named Seymour Hicks let the otherwise uncredited twenty-four-year-old Hitchcock finish Hicks's picture *Always Tell Your Wife.*

Hired next by the Balcon-Freeman-Saville studio, he acted as assistant director, screenwriter, and art director for his first film, *Woman to Woman,* where he also renewed his acquaintance with a member of the crew, a former Famous Artists editor named Alma Reville. Their friendship blossomed into love, and they became engaged in 1925, the same year Hitchcock made his first (completed) films, *The Pleasure Garden* and *The Mountain Eagle.* The following year when the couple married, he made *The Lodger.* The film was a major success and launched his career in England, one that would soon make him the country's most successful and higest-paid director. Several films followed quickly, including *The Farmer's Wife,* made in 1928, the year the couple's daughter Patricia was born (an actress, she would appear in *Psycho* and *Strangers on a Train*).

The following decade would see an amazing string of successful films, several of them classics, that spread his fame worldwide. Among them were 1934's *The Man Who Knew Too Much, The 39 Steps* (1935), *Secret Agent* and *Sabotage* (both 1936), and *The Lady Vanishes*, which won him the Director of the Year award in 1938 from the New York Film Critics Circle.

Hollywood usually knows a good thing when it sees it—especially if it makes money—and clearly Hitchcock was a good thing. After several studios made offers in the late 1930s, he opted to sign a contract with David O. Selznick, whose *Gone With the Wind* broke all records in 1939 (it didn't hurt Selznick's invitation that Hitchcock's agent was his brother Myron Selznick). Hitchcock was interested in Hollywood both because it was, well, Hollywood, the world center of the film industry, and because it was, perhaps for the same reason, technologically light-years ahead of England. He wanted to flex his muscles with the best filmmaking equipment and talent available.

First slated to direct a film about the sinking of the *Titanic*, which fell through, Hitchcock made his American debut with a movie based on a novel by Daphne du Maurier, the Gothic thriller *Rebecca*. It was a huge success; nominated for eleven Oscars in 1940, it won two, including that for Best Picture. It was the only Hitchcock-directed film to bring home the top Academy Award (it was Selznick's only Best Picture Oscar, too. Hitchcock was nominated for Best Director, but lost to John Ford for *The Grapes of Wrath*). Starring Laurence Olivier, Joan Fontaine, and perhaps most memorably, the late Dame Judith Anderson as the evil Mrs. Danvers, the film consistently appears on "100 Best Films" lists.

This success was followed by a string of hits, among them *Foreign Correspondent* (1940) and several noir-like films, including 1941's *Suspicion*, with Cary Grant and Joan Fontaine; 1943's *Shadow of a Doubt*, ranked by many as the director's best American film and his personal favorite; the classic *Spellbound* (1945), which starred Gregory Peck and Ingrid Bergman and included a famous dream sequence designed by Salvador Dali; and 1946's *Notorious*, starring Grant and Bergman.

The director's contract was expiring about the time he made *The Paradine Case* in 1947 (starring Peck, Charles Laughton, and other Hollywood luminaries, including Ethel Barrymore, the soap-opera-like story was adapted by Hitchcock's wife from a Robert Hichens novel), and by then he was getting tired of having a micro-manager like Selznick involving himself in every detail of his work. Hitchcock's solution was not successful, however. With a friend he formed a company named Transatlantic Pictures, where he made 1948's *Rope*, and *Under Capricorn* (uncharacteristically for Hitchcock, a historical melodrama) the following year. After the company folded, Hitchcock joined Warner Bros., where he would make several of his classic films.

The first was 1951's *Strangers on a Train*, followed by the famous murder-thriller *Dial 'M' for Murder* in 1954, starring Grace Kelly and Ray Milland, unforgettable as a genteel man who icily plans to murder his wife for her money. As frightening as it was, *Dial 'M'* was completely trumped by Hitchcock's next film, *Rear Window*, made the same year for Paramount, the company he started with a generation earlier. Memorably starring James Stewart and Grace Kelly, it has endured as one of the all-time most popular thrillers ever made. Anecdotes abound on its making, too. Among them that Hitchcock had personally chosen Raymond Burr to play the Lars Thorwald character because he looked like David O. Selznick (with whom the director was then on the outs), and that the romance between Kelly and Stewart was inspired by the real-life romance between *Life*'s famed photographer Robert Capa and Ingrid Bergman.

From a technical standpoint, Hitchcock (who directed the film entirely from inside Stewart's apartment, cueing actors via flesh-colored earphones) did something quite unusual for an era when a signature of a big movie was its big sound score (it still is; in fact, many attribute a large percentage of a film's success today to the power of its score). All of the sound in *Rear Window* is diegetic, meaning that all the music, speech, and other sounds come from within the world of the movie itself. Franz Waxman's score recycles music he wrote for earlier films, including *A Place in the Sun* (1951) and *Elephant Walk* (1954), and the songs heard in the background are all from earlier Paramount features, including *Captain Carey, U.S.A.* and *Mr. Music* (both made in 1950) and *Red Garters* (1954).

The next film Hitchcock made (also for Paramount, the following year) was *To Catch a Thief*, starring Cary Grant and Grace Kelly. The same year, 1955, was also the year he became an American citizen and the year he launched his television series *Alfred Hitchcock Presents.* Compared to what went before and what would come, *To Catch a Thief* has been called "Hitchcock-Lite," a film of little content, but filled with style and done with "flick-of-the-wrist ease," according to one reviewer. Noel Coward, a master of the sophisticated, light comedy, called it "Hitchcock Champagne"; nevertheless, we see traces of its frothy mixture of crime and romance in such television series as *Remington Steele* and *Moonlighting.*

*Alfred Hitchcock Presents* lasted seven years, until 1962, and was succeeded by *The Alfred Hitchcock Hour,* which lasted three more. Together, as mentioned earlier, they made him a household name and his portly frame a familiar image. But for film lovers the three films he made during the early television years would, with *Rear Window,* rate as his four great masterpieces: *Vertigo,* made in 1958, *North by Northwest* the following year, and in 1960 one of the most famous and memorable films ever made (and, also, because he primarily utilized his television crew to make it, one of Hitchcock's lowest-budget films), *Psycho.*

Things began going downhill a bit after that. He starred Tippi Hedren in 1963's *The Birds* and again in 1964 in *Marnie.* Astonishingly, for Hitchcock at this point in his career, it was a commercial failure, as were his two succeeding films, *Torn Curtain* in 1966 and *Topaz* in 1969.

The year before making *Topaz,* Hitchcock was presented with both the Irving G. Thalberg Award (for a lifetime of excellent films) and the Directors Guild of America's Lifetime Achievement Award. These awards, given in the director's sixty-ninth year, showcased a certain irony: although Hitchcock's films had been nominated for fifty-two Oscars (winning six), Hitchcock himself, although nominated for five Best Director Oscars (*Rebecca, Lifeboat, Spellbound, Rear Window, Psycho*), never won one. One observer suggested this might have been in the back of his mind when, accepting the Thalberg Award from the Academy, he gave a speech consisting of exactly two words: "Thank you."

In 1972 he returned to England to make *Frenzy,* and four years later was back in Hollywood, making what would be his final film: *Family Plot.* He had started pre-production work on *The Short Night* in 1979—the same year he was awarded the American Film Institute's Lifetime Achievement Award and was knighted by Queen Elizabeth II. However, because of his ill health, the project was dropped.

"Hitch" died on April 29, 1980.

Although they were friends (and committed Communists), Bertolt Brecht (left), then considered "the German Shakespeare," and Lion Feuchtwanger, the man who pioneered the historical novel, lived very different lives. Unlike Feuchtwanger, Brecht, who would write some of his most celebrated works during his time in California (including an English version of his play *Galileo*, written with Charles Laughton, and 1943's *The Good Woman of Setzuan*), only scraped by financially in the film capital before returning to Germany in 1947.

# 6

# The Odd Man Out

## *Bertolt Brecht*

Bertolt Brecht, then considered the "German Shakespeare," arrived in Los Angeles in 1941, fleeing the ever increasing reach of Nazism in Europe. He was also seeking work. Over the six subsequent years, the poet-playwright became a fixture—in fact, an icon to many—of the refugee community. Unlike most of the new arrivals, however, as far as Hollywood was concerned, he was a fish completely out of water.

But to the theater world's everlasting credit, while he was here, he and the great actor Charles Laughton somehow cobbled out an English-language version of his 1935 play *Galileo* (Brecht spoke little English; Laughton spoke no German). Starring Laughton, the play opened a then celebrated production at the Coronet Theater near Beverly Hills on July 31, 1947, before moving on to Broadway five months later. It was directed by Joseph Losey, who was blacklisted in 1951 by the House Un-American Activities Committee.

Brecht's problem, as far as the Hollywood establishment was concerned, was his politics, publicly delivered in works that projected a fierce social criticism. In fact, Brecht never saw the New York production of *Galileo*, as he left the United Sates on October 31, 1947, following his testimony before the same House of Representatives committee that later blacklisted Losey. He was one of nineteen witnesses who joined forces in an attempt to stop the witch hunt then going on in America.

Like many during the 1920s, Brecht had developed a violently anti-bourgeois attitude that reflected his generation's deep disappointment in the civilization that had come crashing down at the end of World War I. Not surprisingly, among his friends were members of the Dadaist group, who through derision and iconoclastic satire aimed at destroying what they condemned as the false standards of bourgeois art. Unlike many of them, he succeeded as a poet and theatrical reformer whose epic theater developed drama as a social and ideological forum for leftist causes.

That's fine if your audience is in agreement with what you are saying; unfortunately, Hollywood built its success on being the capital of bourgeoise culture. In Europe, there were cultural—if controversial—niches for Brecht's talent from the beginning of his career. His early plays, such as *Baal* (1919) and *Drums in the Night* (1922), examples of nihilistic expressionism, caused riots at their openings, bringing Brecht instant notoriety. In 1928 he provided the composer Kurt Weill with the socially bitter libretto for *The Three Penny Opera*, and two years later for Weill's subsequent opera, *The Rise and Fall of the City of Mahagonny,* set in a decadent fictional Southern California. (Weill, with his wife Lotte Lenya, fled Nazi Germany in 1933, eventually settling not in Hollywood, but in Nyack, New York.) About this time, unsurprisingly, Brecht became a committed Communist (which he denied at the House Un-American Activities Committee hearing), mentored by Karl Korsch, an eminent Marxist theoretician who had been a Communist member of the Reichstag.

After Brecht, a Jew, fled Germany for Paris and Scandinavia (mainly Denmark), his books were burned and his citizenship revoked. For the next eight years he and his wife, Helene Weigel, a theater actress, remained in exile before moving on Finland (where he would write *The Resistible Rise of Arturo Ui*, a parable play about Hitler's rise set in depression-era Chicago), England, and then, in 1941, Hollywood. Although he was welcomed by many in the German-speaking community in Southern California, because of the resistance of the film industry establishment, the couple was forced to scrape by in a small house on Twenty-fifth Street in Santa Monica, for which they paid $48.50 a month in rent. He wrote about the disillusioning experience in a short, bittersweet poem:

> Every morning I earn my bread,
> I go to the market, where lies are bought.
> Full of hope,
> I join the ranks of the sellers.

He never really did find the buyers of "lies," but through fellow German refugees he managed to find some film work, albeit marginal. With his friend and frequent host, the historical novelist Lion Feuchtwanger, Brecht co-authored a film play, *Simone,* for Samuel Goldwyn. It was never produced. Nor was a historical film project, *Edouard II*, also written with Feuchtwanger. And with the then famous director Fritz Lang, he collaborated on the 1943 film *Hangmen Also Die.* The co-writer billing would be his only professional Hollywood credit.

Ironically, despite—maybe because of—Brecht's rejection by Hollywood, theatrical posterity would be the winner. Although cut off from the German theater world that nurtured him, besides translating *Galileo,* Brecht would write some of his plays, essays, and poems while in the film capital. Notable among them was 1943's *The Good Woman of Setzuan,* a parable play set in prewar China.

Eugen Bertolt Friedrich Brecht was born February 10, 1898, in Augsburg, Germany, and would spent the first twenty-five years of his life within its Bavarian surroundings. His parents were Sophie and Bertolt Friedrich Brecht, a paper factory worker who eventually advanced to become the company's business manager.

He was a good student, but having failed to "educate his teachers" (as he put it), Brecht began to write occasional poems. In 1914 he had a short play, *Die Bibel* (The Bible), published in the school journal;

this first drama, a kind of Judith story set in the religious wars of the seventeenth century, was the beginning of a lifelong critical involvement in the conflicting teachings of the Bible, influenced, perhaps, by having a Protestant father and a Catholic mother. By the time he was sixteen years old, young Bertolt had already published, to the envy of his classmates, several successful poems (most under the name Bertolt Eugen). From 1917 until 1921 Brecht studied medicine at the University of Munich, but his studies were interrupted during the first year when he served as a paramedic at an army hospital in Augsburg.

In 1923 he was appointed production director at the Munich Kammerspiele; in 1924 at the Deutsches Theater. From then on, he worked as a playwright in Berlin, where the premiere of Weill's *The Threepenny Opera* made him a worldwide celebrity. During his Berlin years, Brecht would also work briefly with the director Max Reinhardt, who was to make headlines in Hollywood in 1934 with a famous production of Shakespeare's *A Midsummer Night's Dream* at the Hollywood Bowl.

During these years, Brecht, by now a passionate Marxist, developed a special form of drama, called "epic theater," where he utilized a technique known as the "alienation effect." This technique—involving his audiences with the past events portrayed in the plays instead of, as was more common, building an emotional attachment with the characters—would make viewers more receptive to Brecht's social and political rhetoric. He also purposely avoided any dramatic structure and utilized a full panorama of acting, music, stage design, and technology techniques to convey his message. One example of the style is Brecht's 1930 play *Joan of the Stockyards*, like Jean Anouilh's later play *L'Alouette* (1953) a humanistic portrayal of Joan of Arc, but in Brecht's case celebrating the proletariat and set in Chicago during the 1920s.

If ever a wife was a soulmate, it was Helene Weigel. Born in Vienna on May 12, 1900, she began what was then known as an "artistic" education in 1915 and got her first theater jobs in 1918 at Frankfurt's

Neues Theater and Berlin's Staatliches Schauspielhaus and Deutsches Theaters. She and Bertolt met in the early 1920s, and they had the first of four children in 1924 (the couple was married in 1929). She also appeared as a factory worker in the 1926 film *Metropolis*, made by the legendary director Fritz Lang, with whom they would reunite in Hollywood (Lang arrived in Hollywood in 1934 at the invitation of David O. Selznick and became an American citizen the following year). After moving to Hollywood, she was hardly more successful than her husband, appearing only once in film as an uncredited janitress in 1944's *The Seventh Cross*, which starred Spencer Tracy as a Jew who escapes a Nazi prison camp and is aided by Hume Cronyn and his wife, Jessica Tandy, as well as Agnes Moorehead, among others; it was directed by the early émigré Fred Zinnemann, who would go on to direct *High Noon* eight years later, followed by *From Here to Eternity* in 1953.

Like Bertolt Brecht, Helene Weigel was politically committed and joined the Communist Party in 1930. Theater was the hub of her life, and she had a major influence on Brecht's literary women characters. She also was famed for their portrayal, most notably the mother in his 1932 play *Die Mutter* and later in *Mother Courage and Her Children*.

After leaving the United Sates in 1947, the couple spent a year in Zurich and in 1949 went to Berlin to help stage *Mother Courage* at Reinhardt's old Deutsches Theater in the Soviet sector (Helene Weigel played the title part, as she would do in an unfinished film made in 1955 co-starring Simone Signoret). This led to the couple's settling in East Berlin and the formation of their own company, the Berliner Ensemble, which Helene directed until her death in May 6, 1971, as well as starring in many celebrated productions. Henceforward the Ensemble and the staging of his own plays had first claim on Brecht's time.

As in Hollywood, after his return to Germany Brecht never really fit in. Many in Eastern Europe found him controversial because of his unorthodox aesthetic theories, and, of course, given the tenor of the times, he was often boycotted in the West for his Communist opinions and membership in the Academy of Arts of the (Communist) German Democratic Republic. He was also torn over his commitment to Communism by the June 1953 uprising in East Berlin that was ruthlessly put down by the Soviet military, yet two years later he received the Stalin Peace Prize.

He died on August 14, 1956, due to a heart attack.

Among the most brilliant satirists of the twentieth century, Aldous Huxley, the author of the classic science-fiction novel *Brave New World*, came to Hollywood because of his pacifist convictions and a conviction that the climate would help his failing eyesight. In the film capital he would continue his success, writing a number of screenplays, the utopian novel *Island*, and earning a reputation as a socially conscious "intellectual's intellectual." In 1971 he published *The Doors of Perception*, a study of consciousness expansion, which made him a guru of the hippie movement (members of the rock group the Doors chose the band's name from the title of his book).

# 7

# The Pacifists

## *Aldous Huxley and Christopher Isherwood*

Aldous Huxley was recognized from an early age as a brilliant satirist, a talent that would be first demonstrated as early as 1921 in his witty criticism of society, the novel *Chrome Yellow*. A decade later he published *Brave New World*, which, as is well-known to its millions of readers, is a very dark vision of a future technocratic society (although, written before Hitler and Stalin really got going, it is not as dark a vision as George Orwell's *1984*, written in 1949 when we knew of Hitler's horrors and began to suspect Stalin's).

A British citizen, Huxley came to California in 1937, not specifically because of fear of Nazi persecution (although he and his family were living in France at the time), but because he believed the climate would help his eyesight, nearly destroyed when he was seventeen by keratitis punctata. And, like his friend Christopher Isherwood who emigrated to Los Angeles two years later, he also came because of his pacifist beliefs.

He would be highly successful in Hollywood—at least compared with many of the other émigrés—and he was delighted with the vitality and generosity he found in his adopted country. But he was disappointed in how that vitality was exercised "in places of public amusement, in dancing, and motoring. Nowhere, perhaps, is there so little conversation," he wrote. "It is all movement and noise like water gurgling out of a bath—down the waste. Yes, down the waste."

Of course, he wasn't the first, nor was he the last to feel that way about American culture. And, obviously, there is more than a little tint of British elitism in his opinion, not unlike a similar elitism exercised by many of the German-speaking refugees. Yet if you looked in the right direction, you could find all the examples of what H. L. Mencken called the "booboisie." And, of course, you still can in recent comments by some rising stars whose knowledge of the world clearly lags far behind their knowledge of, say, hairstyles.

A superficial judgment might suggest that Huxley's 1939 novel *After Many a Summer Dies the Swan* is a condemnation of Hollywood as a materialistic wasteland. Nevertheless, how does one explain that among his screenplays (including two versions of *Brave New World* and one each of his novels *Eyeless in Gaza*, *Point Counter Point*, and *Ape and Essence*) is the very mainstream 1940 adaptation of Jane Austen's *Pride and Prejudice* (which starred Laurence Olivier), 1944's *Jane Eyre* (co-written with John Houseman), and, of all things, an original screenplay for Walt Disney, albeit the appropriately satirical film (given his mind-set) *Alice in Wonderland*?

Perhaps the answer can be found in Huxley's dramatically contrasted background. A member of the British upper class, with its rigid class structure, he lacked the funds to live like one. Although nearly blind, he enjoyed a hugely successful career as a writer of novels, poems, plays, essays on philosophy, arts, sociology, religion, morals, and even travel books. And, as a pacifist, he lived in an era when World War II would cause the death of twenty million Russians, six million Jews, millions of others, and the threat of cataclysmic destruction was made real by the development of the atomic and hydrogen bombs.

Aldous Leonard Huxley was born in Godalming, Surrey, on July 26, 1894, into a family that had many illustrious members. His grandfather, Thomas Huxley, was a famous biologist who assisted Charles Darwin in the development of the theory of evolution. His father, Leonard, was a biographer, editor, and poet. And his mother, Julia, was the sister of a novelist, the niece of the poet Matthew Arnold, and the granddaughter of a famous educator, Thomas Arnold, who became a character in Thomas Hughes's then hugely popular novel *Tom Brown's Schooldays.*

In 1908, the year his mother died, the fourteen-year-old Aldous entered Eton College, Berkshire, where, originally wanting to be a scientist, he studied for five years. His schooling was interrupted in 1910 by the keratitis attack that totally blinded him for eighteen months before his eyesight partially returned. By using special glasses he was able to read, and he also learned Braille. Despite the condition, he continued his studies at Balliol College, Oxford, where he became a close friend of D. H. Lawrence. (He received a first honors in English in 1916, doing much of his reading with the aid of a magnifying glass.)

Because of his blindness, Huxley was unfit for World War I military service, and he turned to writing. His first book of poetry appeared in 1916, and two more volumes soon followed. For a time, he returned to Eton as a teacher, and among his students was Eric Blair, who would, under the pseudonym of George Orwell, write *1984* and *Animal Farm.* A less formal, but nonetheless important part of Huxley's education was his regular attendance at salons hosted by Lady Ottoline Morrell, a socialite and art patron.

Like similar salons he would later patronize in Los Angeles hosted by Salka Viertel, Morrell's provided the many literary, artistic, and political reformers of the era the opportunity to meet and exchange ideas. She surrounded herself with the most important writers and thinkers of her time, and was the inspiration for Lady Bidlake in Huxley's *Point Counter Point*, as well as Hermione Roddice in D. H. Lawrence's *Women in Love* and Lady Caroline Bury in Graham Greene's *It's a Battlefield*. Huxley's gift for satire and cynical view of human nature has been attributed by many to his early exposure to the ideas of such a diverse and progressive group; in Morrell's salon

Huxley met, among others, the novelist Virginia Woolf, the economist John Maynard Keynes, and the legendary philosopher and social critic Bertrand Russell.

In 1919, two years before he wrote *Chrome Yellow*, he married Maria Nys, a Belgian, and the following year their son, Matthew, was born. During the next decade *Chrome Yellow* was followed by a dozen successful books (including, as noted, *Point Counter Point* and *Do What You Will*). Their brilliant dialogue, cynical outlook (certainly appropriate to the 1920s), and social criticism made him both fashionable and financially fairly comfortable.

Huxley spent most of that decade outside England, traveling in France and staying in Italy for long periods. There he experienced Mussolini's Fascist policies (among them the dictator fought against birth control, not for religious reasons but because he needed manpower for wars he saw coming), and many literary scholars have found such influences in Huxley's signature dystopia (an imaginary place in a work of fiction where the characters lead dehumanized, fearful lives).

Influences from his childhood have also been traced in his work, including the social separateness he felt due to his superior intelligence and his deep sense of the transitory nature of human happiness occasioned by his mother's early death. Much of this is especially evident in *Brave New World*, which he wrote in Sanary-sur-Mer in the south of France where the family settled in 1930, the same year his friend Lawrence died in nearby Vence on the Riviera.

As it turned out, the small Provencal town was the place to be if you were planning to flee metropolitan Europe, but when the Huxleys moved there, that was the last thing on their minds. As it turned out, Sanary was popular because—as with Hollywood—others were already there (the Lion Feuchtwangers would live there for seven years before being imprisoned), and it was charming and a place where they could be more or less free while not forsaking Europe. There is a plaque in the town commemorating THE GERMAN AND AUSTRIAN WRITERS WHO WITH THEIR FAMILY AND FRIENDS FLED THE NATIONAL-SOCIALIST REGIME AND

FOUND SAFETY IN SANARY-SUR-MER. Among the names it bears are Franz Werfel, Ludwig Marcuse, Stefan Zweig, and the entire Mann family. Eventually, worsening conditions prompted all of them to flee.

One of Aldous Huxley's first stops in America when he and Maria arrived in 1936 was Taos, New Mexico, already known as an artist's and writer's colony. D. H. Lawrence and his German-born wife Frieda moved there in 1922. There, not far from the site of *Brave New World*'s Savage Reservation, he finished his pacifist work *Ends and Means* before moving on to Los Angeles.

After his move to the United States, Huxley concentrated more on essay writing than fiction, although in 1952 he published *The Devils of Loudon*, a horrifying tale of mass hysteria and exorcism set in seventeenth-century France that attacks the hypocrisy of organized religion (it was made into an equally scarifying opera by the composer Krzysztof Penderecki in 1969). Two years later he wrote *The Doors of Perception*, a landmark study of consciousness expansion through the use of mescaline; it made him the virtual guru of the hippy movement (he took the title from a line in a poem by the mystic William Blake; the famous rock group The Doors then took the name of their band from the title of Huxley's book). At the time Huxley also started to use LSD and became a vegetarian.

The year 1958 saw the publication of *Brave New World Revised*, a series of essays that Huxley said was written because, in writing the earlier work twenty-seven years before, he had failed to recognize the ominous peril of nuclear fission, which he believed brought individual freedom closer to extinction than he previously imagined. The following year's *Brave New World Revisited* was a sequel to the first novel in which he compared the predictions of the earlier book with later developments in science and society. Still mining the lode of social cynicism, he followed this in 1962 with his last novel, the utopian *Island*. In it, a journalist discovers a happy people on a fabled island, only to find that paradise is not immune to the realities of the oil industry. It was written a year after a brushfire destroyed his home in the Hollywood Hills and virtually all his papers except for the *Island* manuscript (during the war, he and Maria moved to a clapboard house in the Mojave Desert, returning when they ran out of money and David Selznick asked him to work on *Jane Eyre*). In 1963 *Literature and Science*, a collection of essays, was published.

A generation earlier, in 1938, soon after Huxley arrived in California, he met and became close to Jiddu Krishnamurti, today recognized as one of the greatest philosophical minds of the twentieth century. Huxley became a follower of Swami Prabhavananda, founder of the Vedanta Society of Southern California. Soon after fellow pacifist Christopher Isherwood's arrival the following year, Huxley introduced him to the group and became active himself in the religion, which is based on the foundation of Hinduism (the Vedanta Temple still stands in Hollywood; unfortunately, the nearby apartment where Isherwood lived for a time before moving to Santa Monica Canyon was torn down to make way for the Hollywood Freeway in 1940).

Not long afterward Huxley wrote *The Perennial Philosophy*, in which he presented the teachings of several of the world's great mystics. He had also heard of the Bates Method for vision improvement and, after being taught how to employ it, claimed his vision was greatly strengthened and wrote a book about it in 1942, *The Art of Seeing*.

In 1955, Huxley's wife Maria died of breast cancer, and the following year he married Laura Archera, herself an author who wrote a biography of Huxley.

Several years later, before writing *Island*, Huxley was diagnosed with throat cancer; nevertheless, he maintained a busy schedule as a lecturer for some time. In 1959, the MacMillian government in Great Britain offered him a knighthood, but he turned it down (he never became a U.S. citizen because, to qualify, he would have to attribute his pacifism to a religious conviction, which he refused to do).

His death became famous for its timing—like the Irish writer C. S. Lewis, he died on November 22, 1963, the day President John F. Kennedy was assassinated. In the end, it was reported, unable to speak, Huxley had given his wife a note asking for a large dose of LSD. She provided it, and he died peacefully.

Today, although not held in quite the same awe he was in his later years, Aldous Huxley is recognized as an intellectual's intellectual, a man who, because of circumstances, was forced to churn out essay after essay and book after book, but one who never lost the social consciousness of his youth.

•••••••

Christopher Isherwood's best-known fictional work is, as many people know, *The Berlin Stories*. Based on long visits to the German capital between 1929 and 1933, it is, in actuality, a pair of loosely structured novels: *Mr. Norris Changes Trains*, written in 1935, and *Goodbye to Berlin*, written in 1939. The reason for the popularity of the works—then and now—is his depiction of the glittering and somewhat grotesque metropolis of the Weimar Republic in its pre-Hitler years: its cafés, night people, and manifold vices. *Goodbye to Berlin* is considered among the most significant political novels of the twentieth century, and in it appears the most popular of the characters in all of Isherwood's books: the joyfully amoral nightclub singer who embodies the carefree individualism of the time and place: Sally Bowles. The book's gay male protagonist, an aspiring writer who tries to keep up with Sally's abandoned lifestyle, is based, like the main character in many of Isherwood's novels, on Isherwood himself. He would also include many of his friends in his books under assumed names, among them W. H. Auden, the writer Stephen Spender, and Virginia Woolf.

In 1951, more than a decade after Isherwood had moved to America, his friend John Van Druten wrote the play *I Am a Camera*, based on the *Berlin* books, which starred Julie Harris as Sally Bowles and William

Christopher Isherwood in later life, relaxing in his library. In the late 1930s he wrote *The Berlin Stories*, which evoked the bohemian life of pre–World War II Berlin. They were later made into the play *I Am a Camera* and the famous musical (and movie) *Cabaret*. Unlike most of the Los Angeles émigrés, he left Europe not because of Nazi persecution, but because of his pacifist convictions.

Prince as Isherwood during its eight-month Broadway run. Harris, along with Lawrence Harvey, who replaced Prince in the Broadway production, starred in the 1955 film of the play. In 1966 the John Kander/Fred Ebb musical *Cabaret*, directed by Hal Prince, based on the *Berlin* books and the play, opened on Broadway; it would run for 1,166 performances. Made into a movie in 1972 directed by Bob Fosse, *Cabaret* won eight Oscars, including one for Liza Minelli, who starred as Sally Bowles (Michael York played the Isherwood role under the name of Brian Roberts, and Joel Grey memorably played the master of ceremonies of the cabaret, the Kit Kat Club).

After immigrating from England in 1939 with the poet W. H. Auden, Isherwood settled in Southern California. There he would write for films, teach, and write several more books, including *Christopher and His Kind*, an autobiography of his life in the 1930s in which he examines his complex relationship with Auden, who died four years before the book was published in 1977.

Other than for *Diane* (with Lana Turner, 1956) and 1965's *The Loved One* (with an all-star cast, adapted from Evelyn Waugh's novel satirizing the funeral industry in Southern California at the time), Isherwood's film work was largely uncredited. Untypically—at least in Hollywood—he apparently didn't mind; basically, Isherwood did it for the income. Nevertheless, until his two-and-a-half-percent royalties started rolling in from Van Druten's play, he was living a somewhat rootless, hand-to-mouth existence, moving from residence to residence, from a room over Salka Viertel's Santa Monica Canyon home to an ocean-view house in Laguna, interrupted by a months-long sojourn in South America and a long stay at a Quaker hostel in Pennsylvania, where he worked with European refugees in 1941 and '42, plus occasional trips to London and New York.

But wherever he was living, Los Angeles was by then his creative and, for the most part, physical home, and it would be for the rest of his life. And the people with whom he associated—other than a series of lovers, including the artist Don Bachardy, whom he met in 1953 when Bachardy was eighteen and who would remain Isherwood's lover for the rest of the writer's life (the pair were painted memorably by David Hockney in 1968)—would be drawn mostly from the refugee and émigré population of the film capital.

Christopher William Bradshaw-Isherwood was born August 26, 1904, in Disley, Cheshire, England. Like many of his literary contemporaries, his parents were comfortably well-off, middle-class but edging slightly toward the aristocratic via the family ownership, dating from the sixteenth century, of a great Elizabethan mansion, Marple Hall, which stood in a huge, waterlogged park. Unfortunately, as Christopher's father, Frank Bradshaw-Isherwood, was the second son of the head of the family and the estate would pass entirely to his older brother on his father's death, Frank Bradshaw-Isherwood would have to earn a living on his own. He chose to become a professional soldier, and when Isherwood was a small child, he would occasionally travel with his father's York and Lancaster regiment. Frank, however, was killed on May 8, 1915, at the second battle of Ypres. Christopher's mother, Kathleen, the daughter of a wine merchant (thus, "in trade" and looked down on by the upper classes), outlived her husband by forty-five years and was determined to uphold class distinctions, ironically at the very time when, because of war and social changes, they were disintegrating. (Near the end of her life she saw the destruction of Marple Hall itself to make way for a school and housing development, with roads called "Bradshaw" and "Isherwood" among them.)

In 1914 Christopher was sent to St. Edmund's Preparatory School, where he made friends with the future poet, W. H. Auden. Later he recalled these days in 1938's *Lions and Shadows*: "I had arrived at my public school thoroughly sick of masters and mistresses, having been emotionally messed about by them at my preparatory school, where the war years had given full licence to every sort of dishonest cant about loyalty, selfishness, patriotism, playing the game and dishonoring the dead."

Isherwood continued his education at Repton School, and in 1925 at Corpus Christi, Cambridge, without taking a degree. After Cambridge he worked for a time as a secretary to André Mangeot, a French violinist, and earned his living also as a private tutor. His first novels, 1928's *All the Conspirators* and *The Memorial* (1934), explored the English middle-class world of the 1920s (the character of Lily Vernon in *The Memorial* is actually a fictionalized portrait of his mother and satirizes her hypocritical snobbery). From 1930 to 1933 Isherwood taught English in Germany while, of course, he was observing the culture that he would famously portray in his *Berlin Diaries*.

In 1945 he wrote *Prater Violet*, a satire of filmmaking in prewar London that drew extensively on his experience working with Salka Viertel's husband, Berthold, in 1933. *The World in the Evening* (1954) is a study of a young writer drawn between two marriages and his homosexuality. *A Single Man* (1964) presents a single day in the life of a lonely, middle-aged homosexual whose partner dies, and in 1972's *Kathleen and Frank* he composed a portrait of his parents from their letters to each other.

Soon after Isherwood's arrival in Hollywood, the Irish writer Gerald Heard introduced him to Vedantism, a religion based on the four Vedas forming the basis of Hinduism. At the time, Isherwood, nominally an atheist, was wrestling with the meaning of his life. "I'm tired of strumming on that same old harp, the Ego, darling me," he wrote to a friend. He was intrigued by what he heard about a different level of consciousness that could be acquired through Vedanta and asked to be introduced to the Swami Prabhavananda, the Indian monk who established a center for the study of Vedanta in Hollywood in 1929. A decade later, about the time Isherwood arrived, Prabhavananda had managed to erect a small onion-domed temple on what is now Vedanta Place off Ivar that remains the center of the religion's presence in the film capital.

As he came to know Prabhavananda, Isherwood became a Vedantist. An integral aspect of Vedantan philosophy particularly appealed to Isherwood: "In the religious outlook on life," he wrote, "you try to see individuals as children of God, rather than just tiresome and often rather hostile freaks. Isn't that what you do in writing really? You see them as children of art, and, in the eye of art, everything is ultimately forgiven." It may be that this logic of compassion within the Vedantan philosophical framework allowed him to accept—without guilt—both his pacifism and his homosexuality.

He remained a Vedantist for the rest of his days. From spring 1942 until March 1944, Isherwood collaborated with Prabhavananda on a translation of the Bhagavad-Gita, actually moving into the monastery adjoining the temple for a time. Later he wrote a biography of Ramakrishna, the nineteenth-century spiritual thinker whose teachings still inspire thousands. In 1980 he composed a spiritual autobiography, *My Guru and His Disciple*, in which the values of Vedanta Hinduism counter his life as a Hollywood screenwriter.

From 1959 to 1962 Isherwood taught as a guest professor at Los Angeles State College and the University of California at Santa Barbara. In 1965 to 1966 he taught at the University of California at Los Angeles. In 1975 he won the Brandeis Medal for Fiction. Because his writing was so explicitly autobiographical and because of his international standing, with the evolution of gay rights after the 1969 Stonewall riots in New York, Isherwood more or less automatically became a leading spokesman for the cause in his later years.

The title of John Van Druten's play *I Am a Camera* was taken from Isherwood's passage in *Goodbye to Berlin* that reads: "I am a camera with its shutter open, quite passive, recording, not thinking. Recording the man shaving at the window opposite and the woman in the kimono washing her hair. Some day, all this will have to be developed, carefully printed, fixed."

There have been those who regret that Isherwood didn't turn the same camera eye on the social milieu of Hollywood during the years that he lived there and write the definitive novel of the film capital's golden era, as he did in Berlin a generation earlier. Actually, he did, but not in a form that could be commercially exploited as successfully as *The Berlin Dairies*.

In volume 1 of his *Diaries*, published in 1996, he traces his life from the time he sailed with Auden to America in 1939 until 1960. In his notes, he fills page after page with gossipy, often brilliant character sketches of the émigrés with whom he socialized, as well as comments about Los Angeles of the time. Even his friends were not immune to his rapier pen.

Consider the following description of a party at the Huxley home: "The walls are hung with semierotic, fetishist pictures of 'cruel' ladies in boots . . . the living room was so dark that a lady, the first person I spoke to, said: 'Will you please light my cigarette, so I can see your face'?" Or his thoughts on surfers, then as now a ubiquitous Southern California presence: "They are like a different race of beings, beautiful and golden."

So, too, in the opinion of many of his contemporaries was Christopher Isherwood. He died in Santa Monica on January 4, 1986.

The director Otto Preminger in the prime of his life and film career. A refugee from Nazism, he would, ironically, play Nazis in several plays and films. Among them was Billy Wilder's 1953 prison-camp movie *Stalag 17*, made in the same year that Preminger directed his great film *Laura*.

# 8

## The Dictatorial Innovator

### *Otto Preminger*

One of the ironies in Hollywood of the era was the fact that a number of refugees from Nazi persecution were cast in Nazi roles in the propaganda films of the time. We've noted elsewhere the casting of the German refugee Conrad Veidt as the Nazi Major Strasser in *Casablanca*. Another was Otto Preminger, who came to America as a director but was forced to support himself in Hollywood during much of World War II as an actor. And playing Nazis, of course: among them 1942's *The Pied Piper*, released only seven months after Pearl Harbor.

By 1944, Preminger was out of his Nazi (and acting) harness (although he would do his Nazi turn in one more film, Billy Wilder's 1953 classic, Oscar-winning *Stalag 17*) and back on the other side of the camera. That year he directed one of the greatest of the noir films, *Laura* with Gene Tierney, Dana Andrews, Clifton Webb, Vincent Price, and, of course, the great Judith Anderson. It won an Oscar (Best Cinematography) and brought him his first Oscar nomination for directing. It would be followed by thirty-two films in which he explored hitherto taboo subjects such as drug addiction (*The Man With the Golden Arm*, 1955), homosexuality (*Advise and Consent*, 1962), all the while turning out such classics as *Exodus* (1960) and 1953's *The Moon Is Blue* (the first mainstream film to use "virgin" in its dialogue, it was banned in Boston because of its "sexual explicitness," thus provoking the phrase that would be used thereafter to refer to matters thought to be offensive to public sensibilities). All of this controversy made him one of the few directors to become a household name.

Otto Ludwig Preminger was born on December 5, 1905, in Vienna, Austria, to a Jewish family. His father was a prosecutor for the Austro-Hungarian Empire, and Otto originally intended to follow his father into a law career. As a student, however, he decided that the theater—not the law—was his future and, when he was seventeen, like many future Hollywood émigrés and refugees, joined Max Reinhardt's theater company. (Years later in Hollywood he would memorably direct such law-themed films as 1955's *The Court-Martial of Billy Mitchell* and *Anatomy of a Murder*, which won seven Oscars, including the one for Best Picture in 1960.)

In 1925 Preminger became a stage director and eventually succeeded Reinhardt when he went to Hollywood to direct *A Midsummer Night's Dream* at the Hollywood Bowl in 1934 and co-direct the film version made the following year. He directed his first film, *Die Grosse Liebe* (*The Great Love*), in 1931, and the following year when he was only twenty-seven, he was offered an appointment as head of the State Theater in Vienna. Preminger turned the offer down, as it required that he officially convert to the state religion, Catholicism, even though he was nonreligious (Gustav Mahler had no such compunctions when offered the directorship of the Vienna State Opera with a similar condition a generation earlier). From 1933 until 1935, Preminger did, however, remain in Vienna, as the administrator of the Theater der Josefstadt, where he directed many plays, both comedies and dramas.

In 1936 Broadway producer Gilbert Miller invited him to come to New York to stage Edward Wooll's courtroom drama *Libel*; it was so successful that 20th Century Fox offered him a contract. After he arrived, the studio really didn't know what to do with him, using him as both a dialogue coach and as an actor in a couple of films, including *Danger—Love at Work* with Ann Sothern and Jack Haley. In

1938, after an argument with his boss, 20th Century production chief Darryl Zanuck, he was fired from the Freddie Bartholomew version of *Kidnapped* and wouldn't direct again for another five years.

He returned to Broadway as a director and occasional actor, casting himself as a Nazi in Clare Boothe Luce's play *Margin for Error*. Opening only two months after the fall of Poland, it was a hit and, when it was made into a film in 1943, brought him back to Hollywood as a director again. Until then, he continued directing off and on Broadway and, famously, fathered a son, Erik Lee Preminger, with the stripper Gypsy Rose Lee. When Zanuck returned from wartime service, he replaced the director of *Laura*, Rouben Mamoulian, with Preminger, and the rest, as they say, is history.

The success of the film translated into steady work for Preminger the director, and in 1947 he was chosen to direct the studio's notorious *Forever Amber*, an adaptation of Kathleen Windsor's best seller about a young woman who sleeps her way to the top of Restoration England. Despite the fact that the Catholic Legion of Decency gave it a "condemned" rating, Zanuck successfully released the movie without cuts, convincing Hollywood in general and Preminger in particular that there was a huge audience in America for movies with adult themes, a lesson Preminger would follow with his controversial movies (cuts were made, however, when the movie went into release in the Bible Belt).

By then Preminger had established himself as a director of thrillers with *Fallen Angel* (1945), followed by *Whirlpool* (1949), *Where the Sidewalk Ends* (1950), 1951's *The 13th Letter* (1951), and *Angel Face* the following year when he was loaned out to RKO. He was also getting a reputation for being harsh with his actors—while making *Angel Face*, he demanded that Robert Mitchum actually slap his co-star, Jean Simmons, in the face instead of faking it, as was the custom.

In the early 1950s he left Fox to become an independent producer-director, his first picture an adaptation of the then scandalous sex comedy that he had directed on Broadway, *The Moon Is Blue*. It was quickly condemned by Hollywood's censorship board, originally created in response to the public backlash over Hollywood's scandals and the licentiousness of many films made in the 1920s. The Breen Office, as the censor was known, even enforced the morality code against foreign films, denying a seal of approval to Vittorio De Sica's *The Bicycle Thief*, which, on the basis of screenings before the film was submitted for approval, won the Academy Award for Best Foreign Film in 1949.

Most of Hollywood thought that Preminger would not buck the system and risk financial ruin if the picture was released without the censor's approval; they didn't know their man, who went ahead and released it anyway. Although the exhibition of the movie was banned in many cities, the courts soon overturned most of the bans, and when it played, it did so to standing-room-only audiences, grossing $6 million (a phenomenal performance for a film that cost $450,000 to make). Although the Breen Office would last another thirteen years, Preminger's bawdy comedy was the beginning of the end of institutionalized censorship of the movies.

In 1954 Preminger returned to Fox for *River of No Return*, the first western shot in the new CinemaScope wide-screen process. He next made *Carmen Jones*, another challenge to Hollywood's unwritten policy against making movies with all-black casts . . . its star, Dorothy Dandridge, would be the first African-American lead to be nominated for a Best Actress Oscar. (The first African-American to win an Oscar was Hattie McDaniel, who won Best Supporting Actress for *Gone With the Wind*.) It was rumored that at about this time Preminger had offered to marry Dandridge, but walked out on her when she became pregnant, and she had an abortion. Nevertheless, she would star in the Preminger-directed film version of Gershwin's *Porgy and Bess*, which also featured an all-black cast.

Preminger then bought the rights to Nelson Algren's powerful novel about drug addiction, *The Man With the Golden Arm* (1955). Like sex, drug addiction was another subject proscribed by the censors, but

Preminger again was determined to flout the rules; after Marlon Brando turned down the role of the heroin-addicted drummer and cardsharp, Preminger settled for Frank Sinatra, who gave an Oscar-nominated performance that was one of his best. Preminger, once again, released his film without Hollywood's Production Code Administration's Code of Approval, and once again he had a hit, opening the door for a relaxation of the Code the following year.

In 1959 Preminger made what many feel is, after *Laura,* his masterpiece, *Anatomy of a Murder.* Featuring brilliant performances by James Stewart and George C. Scott, the film, which dramatized a rape trial, also ran afoul of censors, again for its blunt language and its (for the times) frank "anatomy" (clinical presentation) of rape. The film's dialogue went far beyond what audiences of the time were accustomed to hearing at the movies. In it he cast as the trial judge the real-life judge Joseph Welch, who as counsel to the army, had brought down the notorious Senator Joseph McCarthy in televised hearings, thus ending the reign of terror still known as McCarthyism.

*Exodus,* made in 1960 and based on Leon Uris's popular novel about the founding of Israel, was the first in a series of blockbuster films Preminger would make during the 1960s. Again he tempted fate by hiring the blacklisted screenwriter Dalton Trumbo to write the script for the film. But it seemed that the bigger canvases occasionally got in Preminger's creative way, films like *The Cardinal,* for instance. The year 1966's *Hurry Sundown*, a film about race relations was, quite simply, a bad movie.

His autocracy was scaring off people, too. In addition to forcing Mitchum to really slap his co-star in *Angel Face*, he fired Lana Turner from *Anatomy of a Murder* when she refused to wear the wardrobe he picked out for her (she was replaced by the then unknown Lee Remick, who received an Oscar nomination for her work). "I say what I like because it is completely my picture, an independent picture," Preminger said at the time. "I am the producer, the director, the casting director, it's all my decision."

Despite some success with movies like 1965's *Bunny Lake Is Missing*, when film made a turn toward a more personal style during the sixties, he couldn't make the adjustment and became, for all his pioneering, passé as far as Hollywood was concerned, and the few films he made after that were embarrassing. Sadly, instead of being allowed to simply fade away, as did many of his colleagues—George Cukor, John Ford, and Howard Hawks—he was reviled by many of the same people who stood in awe when he earlier fought for cinematic freedom. His courage was called stubbornness, and much of his cinematic innovation and craftsmanship was cited as artificial. He died April 23, 1986, in New York City, a victim of cancer and Alzheimer's disease.

A sad ending? Yes, if one considers the physical arc of his career—from success to adulation to being dismissed as a failure. But go and see one of his great films—*Anatomy of a Murder* for one, *Laura* for another . . . or many of the films made between them. They are the legacy of a major artist.

A failure? Hardly.

The Nobel Prize–winning German émigré writer Thomas Mann (center) visits with Mme Luchere-Vallentina at a party, probably at Lion and Marta Feuchtwanger's Pacific Palisades home, as Marta Feuchtwanger (right) looks on. Before returning to Europe in 1952 in disgust over America's McCarthyism, the man fellow émigré Louis Marcuse dubbed "the Emperor of Exiles" would write his last great novel, the controversial *Doctor Faustus*, at his home near the Feuchtwangers'.

# 9

## The Writers

### *Thomas Mann and Lion Feuchtwanger*

O f all the displaced Germans in Los Angeles in the 1940s, none was more famous than the Nobel Prize–winning writer Thomas Mann. Because of his ubiquitous presence and fame, a fellow émigré, Louis Marcuse, dubbed him "The Emperor of the Exiles."

On July 8, 1940, soon after Mann and his wife Katia arrived in Los Angeles, he wrote his friend Erich von Kahler, a professor who fled Germany in 1933, emigrated to the United States in 1938, and settled in Princeton, New Jersey. "We have moved into a rather magnificent, roomy house in a hilly landscape strikingly similar to Tuscany," Mann wrote about the couple's home at 441 North Rockingham in L.A.'s Brentwood suburb (not far from the house made notorious a half century later as the home of O. J. Simpson). "I have what I wanted. [We enjoy] . . . the light, the dry always refreshing warmth, the spaciousness compared with Princeton (where Mann, arriving in 1936, had taught and written before moving on to Southern California), the holm oaks, eucalyptus, cedar, and palm vegetation. The walks by the ocean, which we can reach by car in a few minutes.

"There are some good friends here," he added of refugees and émigrés who arrived earlier. "First of all the Walters [Bruno Walter, the eminent conductor, and his wife, Elsa] and the Franks [Bruno, a famous German author, and his wife, Liesl], besides our two oldest children, and life might be enjoyable were it not that our spirits are too oppressed for pleasure—and for work also as I discovered after some initial attempts. We know nothing about my brother . . . nothing about Golo."

The question about the whereabouts of his elder brother, Heinrich, his sister-in-law, Nelle, and his middle son, Golo, would be answered within three months when, accompanying Franz and Alma Werfel, they arrived, unheralded, in Hoboken, New Jersey, having sailed from Lisbon after a harrowing, months-long walk out of Hitler's Europe.

Like the Werfels and many of the German-American refugees, the Manns tended to socialize more or less solely with their displaced compatriots. "We live our by now deeply habituated waiting room days, among our palms and lemon trees," he wrote. "Always the same faces. And if occasionally an American countenance appears," Mann added, reflecting the elitist attitude of many of the German-speaking arrivals, "it is as a rule so strangely blank and amiably stereotyped that one has had quite enough for some time to come."

Thomas Mann was born June 6, 1875, in the German commercial seaport of Lübeck, making him one of the oldest of the refugees from Nazism. He was the second of five children born to Thomas Johann, a wealthy grain merchant and twice mayor of the city, and Julia da Silva, born in Brazil of a German plantation owner and his Portuguese-Creole wife. When Mann's father died in 1891, his trading firm was dissolved, and the family moved to Munich.

Thomas, however, remained in Lübeck to finish his high school education. Freed of the demand that he follow in his father's mercantile footsteps, the artistically inclined seventeen-year-old turned to literature, which would be his love and career, editing and writing short stories for his school's newspaper while reading voraciously. After graduating, Thomas joined his family in Munich in 1894 and worked for the South German Fire Insurance Company while attending Munich's Technical University, writing in his spare time. Although he had a story published earlier (attracting the attention and support of the writer Richard Dehmel), his career as a writer really started in the magazine *Simplicissimus* in 1896. He began reading Schopenhauer and Nietzsche and immersing himself in the music of Richard Wagner, and moved to Italy with his older brother Heinrich, by then an established writer himself.

There he finished a short story, "The Little Mr. Friedman," which would become the core of his first book (of short stories), and began work on his first novel, *Buddenbrooks*, which would be published soon after his return to Munich in the fall of 1900. A textbook example of the maxim that authors write best about things they know best, *Buddenbrooks* relates the saga of several generations of a merchant family who belong to the bourgeois aristocracy in Lübeck, tracking them from their highest point of eminence through an inevitable decline. Despite outraging the citizens of Lübeck, who rightly saw it as a thinly veiled account of local incidents and figures, the book was an overnight success and made the writer financially comfortable, if not quite rich, by the time he was twenty-five. Writer Henry Hatfield explained what probably gave *Buddenbrooks* its greatest appeal. "In [it], he wrote one of the last of the great 'old-fashioned' novels." Two years later Mann published *Tonio Kroeger*, essentially a spiritual autobiography.

In 1903 Mann met Katia Pringsheim, daughter of a Jewish university mathematician, and despite his homosexual inclinations, he married her. The couple's first child, Erika, arrived that year as well; their first son, Klaus, the next year. The pair were followed by two more daughters, Monika and Elisabeth, and two sons, Golo and Michael. Erika and Klaus were both gay, and, unlike their father, nonconformists. Despite Klaus's fury over Erika's three-year marriage to Gustav Grundgens—later a pillar of Nazi theater life and the subject of Klaus's famous, once banned 1936 novel *Mephisto*, they were inseparable companions (they often claimed to be twins, though there was a year's difference in age between them). In 1936 Erika entered into a marriage of convenience with the gay poet W. H. Auden, with whom she remained (technically) married until her death in 1969. Both Erika and Klaus starred in anti-Fascist cabaret and before and during the war worked as journalists. In 1938 they covered the Spanish Civil War together and the following year wrote *Escape to Life*, a book about German exiles—basically themselves (in 2000 it was made into a docudrama, with the voices of Vanessa and Corin Redgrave as Erika and Klaus Mann).

In 1906 Mann wrote his only dramatic work, *Fiorenza*, which was only a moderate success. Six years later he wrote his celebrated novella "Death in Venice," loosely based on a 1911 visit to Venice. It was made into an opera by Benjamin Britten and in 1971 a movie made by Luchino Visconti, starring Dirk Bogarde and Bjorn Andresen, which *The Atlantic Monthly* magazine critic David Denby reviewed as an insult to both Mann and Gustav Mahler (whose music plays a major part in the film).

Whether or not Mann himself developed a fixation on a beautiful boy, as does his "Death in Venice" protagonist Gustav von Aschenbach, has long been a subject of speculation. But it is known that he modeled many of the characters in the novella on real-life counterparts, among them the story's fourteen-year-old Tadzio, who was inspired by an eleven-year-old, sailor-suited boy named Wladyslaw Moes that Mann saw during his Venetian sojourn.

At the beginning of World War I, Mann, unlike his brother Heinrich who was a supporter of democracy, supported the German monarchy. But as it became clear that Germany would lose the war, he accepted the inevitable and became publicly nonpolitical. Perhaps his dismay over the defeat of his country and convictions affected the pace of his work, but it would be ten years before he completed his next book, *The Magic Mountain*.

During the late 1920s and '30s, as a member of the Prussian Academy of Art, Mann wrote about current events, including worldwide inflation that enabled the rise of Fascism, as well as beginning his three-part Joseph series, a project that would occupy him for nearly two decades.

In 1929 he received the Nobel Prize, primarily for *Buddenbrooks*, published a generation earlier (in a short autobiography written for the Nobel committee, Mann stated that there were still a million copies of the novel in circulation).

Concerned about the rise of Nazism, Mann basically defected during a 1933 European lecture tour, first settling on the French Riviera and then in Zurich, Switzerland. The Nazi regime formally voided his German citizenship in 1936, and the following year the University of Bonn deprived him of his honorary doctorate, awarded in 1919 (the degree was restored in 1946). Mann, who had anticipated and warned against the rise of Fascism during the Weimar Republic (e.g., in 1930's "Mario and the Magician"), continued to combat it in many pamphlets and talks throughout the period of the Nazi regime and the Second World War.

In California, Mann (who became a U.S. citizen in 1940) continued to work on the Joseph novels (the first of the series, dealing with the conflict between personal freedom and political tyranny and based on Genesis 12:50, was published while he was at Princeton) and socialize with his fellow Germans.

In 1947 his last great work, *Doctor Faustus*, was published, and it caused a great deal of turmoil within that tightly knit expatriate group. A reworking of the Faust legend, it tells the story of a composer named Adrian Leverkuhn who sells his soul to the devil for a generation of fame (a metaphor for the destruction of the German culture in the two world wars). Integral to the story of the musician is his modern twelve-tone music system; it didn't take long for Mann's fellow refugee Arnold Schoenberg, the composer who had actually invented twelve-tone music, to decide that the book was actually a personal attack on him. Although Mann later denied this in a 1949 apologia, nevertheless, people believed it at the time, and they still do. It also created terrible problems for socializing within the expatriot community, since the Manns and the Schoenbergs could never be invited to the same event.

Mann was also quite busy accepting a number of awards and honorary doctorates from various American and European institutions. In 1952 Senator Joseph McCarthy's witch hunts drove Mann back to Europe, where he and his wife settled in the Zurich, Switzerland, suburb of Kilchberg. He would remain there the rest of his days, continuing to write, publish, and remain politically active in the affairs of divided cold war Germany until his death.

Thomas Mann, despite all his honors, never really evolved beyond his bourgeois background, which permeates *Buddenbrooks*. It was a bourgeois background that was conservative and, apparently, had the typical Victorian-era horror of emotional display. This aspect of his personality is found in his intellectual, high-toned writing style, which produces a cool distance between the reader and the story. He knew it, too, writing in *The Magic Mountain*: "A man lives not only his personal life as an individual, but also, consciously or unconsciously, the life of his epoch and his contemporaries."

From his *Buddenbrooks* days, Mann used leitmotifs—recurring symbolic phrases—in his writing, clearly inspired by Richard Wagner's development of the technique in his music. But, unlike Wagner, who always valued the motivation of the heart over the logic of the mind, Thomas Mann does just the opposite, often using—and expecting the reader to use—his head in order to reach the heart.

In Mann's life, this unbending view of personal behavior reached a tragic denouement on May 21, 1949, when his son Klaus committed suicide in the south of France. When Mann received news of the death, he was so mortified by the act that he sent a telegram of condolence rather than attend the funeral.

Thomas Mann died August 12, 1955. His wife, Katia, outlived him by twenty-five years, dying at the age of ninety-seven at their home in Switzerland in 1980.

Mann's older brother, Heinrich, was once far more celebrated as a writer, his most successful novel 1904's *Professor Unrat*. It was filmed many times, most famously by Josef von Sternberg in 1930 as *The Blue Angel,* starring Marlene Dietrich. Nevertheless, he was far less successful in Hollywood, and his career illustrates the down side of the refugee experience in the film capital. After his arrival in 1940, Heinrich basically worked out his career as a wage earner, earning $125 weekly during a long stretch with MGM. Of course, one could make the point that Thomas and Katia Mann's Los Angeles lifestyle was financed by his novel writing, and that he never had to turn to Hollywood's movie industry for support, as did Heinrich. It is more or less accepted that Heinrich's comparative failure—compared with fellow German-speaking refugees like Billy Wilder and Fred Zinnemann—was due less to his talent than to the elitist, cold personality he shared with his brother. His wife, Nelle, suffering from mental illness, committed suicide in 1944, and Heinrich died in Santa Monica, California, in 1950.

•••••••

We've mentioned the tension between Thomas Mann and Arnold Schoenberg because of Mann's novel *Doctor Faustus.* Among the many German-speaking hosts who had to be careful not to invite them to the same gathering were Lion and Marta Feuchtwanger.

Of all the high-profile refugees from Hitler's Germany who settled in Southern California, they are among the least remembered, and, other than the fact that their name is hard for many of the English-speaking population to pronounce, it's hard to understand why.

For one thing, Lion Feuchtwanger was a major German historical novelist with a résumé crammed with best-selling works (the fact that none were made into films didn't help his Hollywood reputation though). Among them was 1929's *Success,* a thinly veiled attack about Hitler's rise, and the 1923–42 trilogy Josephus (unlike Mann's Joseph trilogy, based on the biblical Joseph, Feuchtwanger's Josephus was subtitled "The Jewish War" and relates the story of Flavius Josephus, a Jewish historian who lived in Rome in the first century A.D.). Among the books written after Feuchtwanger's arrival in America was 1947's *Proud Destiny*, a novel of the American Revolutionary War.

•••••••

Born on July 7, 1884, in Munich, Germany, Lion was the son of a wealthy Jewish industrialist. At Berlin and Munich universities he studied philosophy, literature, and ancient and modern languages, and also developed a working interest in theater; in fact, while still a student he composed three short plays based on the Old Testament, and after graduation became a drama critic until he took up writing as a full-time profession.

The arrival of Lion and Marta in Southern California was about as highly visible as it could be. When Hitler came to power in 1933, the couple was on a U.S. tour, and they never went back to Germany after learning that their home had been ransacked by Nazi agents. (Because he wrote a sarcastic piece about Hitler in 1927, Lion was later accused by the Nazis of "premature anti-Fascism," his books burned, and his citizenship revoked.) They did return to Europe, though, settling in the south of France, where they eventually ended up in an internment camp. In 1940 President Franklin D. Roosevelt, having come across a photograph of Lion taken in the camp showing him looking frail and sickly, personally arranged through the American journalist Varian Fry, who helped many refugees escape, to have the couple released. After walking across the Pyrenees to Spain, they, like the Werfels and the Heinrich Manns after them, sailed from neutral Lisbon to the United States.

Probably the neglect of this great novelist dated from the late 1940s and 1950s when his Communist sympathies branded him as a "fellow traveler" during the witch hunts of the time. And his naïveté didn't help either. In the midst of the infamous prosecution of many falsely accused individuals, Feuchtwanger made a visit to Moscow and was

After walking across half of Europe to escape Nazism, historical novelist Lion Feuchtwanger and his wife Marta eventually settled in what their neighbor Thomas Mann called "a virtual castle by the sea." Now restored as the Villa Aurora, it is a twenty-room mansion where he wrote six novels (including one about the American Revolutionary War), established a library of thirty-six thousand volumes, and, with his wife, hosted parties for many of the most famous of the exiles.

granted an interview by Stalin because of his political sympathy. His later report on the interview was filled with praise of the Russian dictator and his programs. This taint of Communism was, in fact, fatal to the careers of several refugees, among them the Feuchtwangers' friends Helene and Bertolt Brecht (with whom Lion collaborated on two screenplays).

And those who accepted Feuchtwanger's avowed Communism couldn't understand it; after all, they lived in what Thomas Mann called "a veritable castle by the sea." Gottfried Reinhardt, son of the famous refugee director Max Reinhardt, once said, "I was always amused that this very intelligent, encyclopedically well-read man living in the luxury of a fabulous house with a fabulous library with a fabulous view was really a fanatic communist."

And what a house it was and, thanks to the nonprofit foundation that owns it today, still is. Now called the "Villa Aurora" (the name was given in the 1960s when the neighborhood decided to give itself a Mediterranean flair), the house was designed in 1927 by Mark Daniels, who designed L.A.'s famous Hotel Bel-Air. It was built by the *Los Angeles Times* as a demonstration house designed to attract residents to the then fairly remote Los Angeles suburb of Pacific Palisades. The area, once the site of silent films made by movie pioneer Thomas Ince, is one of the most exclusive in the area, boasting tremendous views from atop a high bluff. The ambiance has often been compared to that of the French Riviera or, with some imagination, Italy's dramatic Amalfi Coast. (The celebrated opera singer Amelita Galli-Curci was a neighbor.)

The villa is a 6,700-square-foot, twenty-room Spanish Revival mansion that, when it was built, boasted such then rare convenience items as a dishwasher, a trash compactor, and an electric garage door opener. Because wartime gasoline rationing and the absence of public transportation severely impacted the area, the Feuchtwangers were able to buy it in 1943 for only nine thousand dollars. And, of course, the enforced remoteness of the place—at least in the beginning while wartime restrictions were in place—was no problem for Feuchtwanger, who sought solitude for his writing; he wrote six novels in his study on the top floor of the house before his death in 1958.

But as much as he loved solitude, Lion liked company—especially that of his fellow refugees and émigrés. The villa soon became one of the major social sites of that part of West Los Angeles, then dubbed "the Weimar of the Pacific" because so many German-speaking refugees and émigrés lived there. The couple often hosted readings from Lion's current novel for an audience that included Bertolt Brecht, Heinrich and Thomas Mann (but never when Schoenberg was there); the Aldous Huxleys, and the writer Franz Werfel and his wife Alma. Afterward everyone would dine on herring salad and apple strudel. Occasionally they would also play darts, using as a target a picture of Adolf Hitler; pockmarked, it still hangs in the office of the director of the foundation that now owns the house.

The Feuchtwangers also often entertained friends at intimate teas, among them Charles and Oona Chaplin, Charles Laughton and his wife Elsa Lanchester, Peter Lorre, the composer Kurt Weill (when he was visiting from his Nyack, New York, home), Albert Einstein, filmmaker Jean Renoir, and modern composer Arnold Schoenberg and his wife Gertrude (again, never with Thomas Mann).

The place was even complete with an organ in the living room, which Arnold Schoenberg played with gusto, and a spectacular 36,000-book library, the third one acquired by the novelist (Lion's first library was burned by the Nazis, and it took some time for the second, left behind when they fled France, to catch up with them).

Bertolt and Helene Brecht were angered by the house, not surprisingly when one considers their political convictions. As Marta Feuchtwanger later recalled, Bertolt, probably jealous comparing the Feuchtwangers' "castle by the sea" to the Brechts' small bungalow, once complained, "How can you move so far away from everything? You can only live in Santa Monica (where the Brechts lived). Pacific Palisades doesn't exist. When somebody's sick, there's no doctor. When you need a pharmacy, there isn't one. You cannot live so far away from civilization." According to Marta, Helene added, "This house looks like a hotel . . . and I wouldn't live in it for everything."

In 1972 Marta told interviewer Lawrence Wechsler: "They [the Brechts] wanted me to give the deed back [but] we couldn't find another house. I was not yet fond of this house because, when this conversation took place, it was still empty.

"I was fond of the idea of the possibility of the garden," she added. Every time my husband got money for his books or from the movies, we didn't buy a fur coat [for me] or a new suit for my husband; he went to the book dealers downtown and I went to the nurseries. I said I planted trees because you make paper out of trees and a writer needs paper. We even had papyrus growing in the garden."

Following the death of her husband, Marta Feuchtwanger bequeathed the house and library to the University of Southern California with the provision that she would live there until her death. After she died in 1987 (at the age of ninety-four) and fearing that the university would sell the villa, a group of concerned Germans and Angelenos soon formed the Friends of Villa Aurora, a group determined to find a way to keep the house and library intact as a cultural monument to German writers and artists who fled the Nazi persecution and settled in Los Angeles. In 1990, with the support of such as novelist Gunther Grass and former German Chancellor Willy Brandt, and the financial help of the Berlin Lottery Foundation and the German government, the group purchased the villa in 1990 for $1.9 million. As part of the deal, the rare books in the library were transferred to the University of Southern California, and some 22,000 volumes were left on the shelves of the house as a permanent loan from the school.

Before the nonprofit Friends of Villa Aurora organization could move in, the villa's sadly deteriorated interior and, more seriously, its crumbling foundation had to be upgraded. It would take three years and $1.6 million more from Germany.

Certainly the Feuchtwangers would be happy with the fate of their home. The foundation it now houses, in addition to fostering a German-American exchange in the fields of literature, art, science, and politics, houses an artists-in-residence program for musicians, writers, filmmakers, journalists, photographers, and other creative persons.

Bruno Walter was one of the most famous and beloved conductors of the last century. Unlike most of his fellow Jews, he originally decided to settle in Hollywood not to escape Nazism (although by the time he finally did so, that was clearly the main reason), but because of the weather. As a protégé, friend, and authoritative interpreter of the music of Gustav Mahler, he had close ties to many of the other émigrés, including, of course, fellow exile Alma Werfel, Mahler's widow. Until his death in 1962, Walter concertized extensively, leaving many recordings as part of his imperishable legacy.

# 10

## The Conductors

### *Bruno Walter and Otto Klemperer*

B runo Walter was one of the most beloved conductors of the twentieth century. An Austrian and formerly assistant to Gustav Mahler, he excelled, naturally, in performing the works of his mentor and similar composers drenched in the romanticism of the era like Anton Bruckner, as well as those of the stylistically far different Wolfgang Amadeus Mozart and Beethoven.

Like most of the émigrés and refugees, he was Jewish and fled Europe because of the Nazi persecution. But unlike most of them, he visited and discovered an affection for Los Angeles—at least the Los Angeles weather—long before they did. "I came to California for the first time in 1927," he said in an interview with *Los Angeles Times* critic Albert Goldberg. "I had to conduct a concert at the Hollywood Bowl, and fell in love with the place at first sight," Walter added. "After that I always wanted to make my domicile here, but only in 1935 could I do so."

By then he hardly had a choice: as a Jew already in America, he certainly would have been disinclined to move back to his native Germany. But why California instead of New York, then the center of America's classical music-making? As we mentioned in our preface, like many other less creatively endowed European immigrants already in Southern California, he was also fleeing "the *allegro furioso* of New York City to the *allegretto grazioso* of Beverly Hills." The weather was better.

That didn't mean he began living in Southern California permanently in 1935—that wouldn't come for four more years. In 1933, when being a Jew in Germany became impossible, he moved to Vienna, which would be his main center of activity for several years, although he was a frequent guest conductor of Amsterdam's Concertgebouw Orchestra between 1934 and the end of the decade when the Nazis invaded the Netherlands. (The music director of the Concertgebouw and ardent advocate of Mahler's music was the celebrated conductor Willem Mengelberg, who later supported the German occupation, for which, after the war, he was banned from ever again conducting in the country.)

During the 1930s Walter frequently conducted the New York Philharmonic and was a guest conductor at the Vienna State Opera until 1938 when the Anschluss, the annexation of Austria into the Third Reich, took place on March 12. Earlier, in 1935, he made a now legendary recording of the first act of Richard Wagner's *Die Walküre* with the Vienna Philharmonic Orchestra and a cast including the great German soprano Lotte Lehmann and the legendary Danish tenor Lauritz Melchior.

Born Bruno Walter Schlesinger in Berlin on September 15, 1876, he began his music education when he was eight and made his first concert appearance the following year (as a pianist). After hearing only two concerts by Hans von Bulow (to whom Richard Wagner's second wife, Cosima Liszt, was then married), he decided on a conducting career.

After being engaged as a coach at the Cologne Opera, he was quickly given conducting responsibilities there and in Hamburg, where he subsequently worked as a chorus director under Mahler, who many music lovers do not realize was, in his day, far more celebrated as a conductor than as a composer (thanks, in part, to Walter's later pioneering recordings of Mahler's music). Walter then joined Mahler at the Vienna Court Opera (he debuted conducting *Aida*), as well as continuing to conduct on his own in Prague, London, and Rome when

Mahler left for the United States and several seasons conducting the New York Philharmonic Orchestra and the Metropolitan Opera.

After Mahler died in 1911, Walter led the first performance of the composer's song cycle *Das Lied von der Erde* (*The Song of the Earth*) in Munich, as well as the first performance of his last symphony (the Ninth) in Vienna. That year he also became an Austrian citizen; he had already formally changed his name to "Walter." Throughout his life and even after his death, some claimed that he changed his Jewish name to further his career, though the story is only partly supported by the facts. When in 1896 (at the instigation of Mahler) he was offered the position of second conductor to the conductor Theodore Loewe at the provincial Breslau, Loewe insisted that he change his name. His reason? There were too many Schlesingers in Breslau (now in Poland).

There is little question that doing so greatly troubled the young musician. He wrote his parents that having to change his name was "terrible," a name not being "just a piece of clothing that you can simply slip off," he said. "It makes you shudder, doesn't it?" But he did it, both for his career and because of the pressure exerted by Mahler and his sisters.

In 1901 he married the soprano Elsa Korneck, and they had two daughters, Lotte in 1903 and Gretel three years later. Eventually the couple moved to Munich, where Walter remained as the Royal Bavarian music director until 1922. It was there, in 1916, that he met the great love of his life (another soprano), Delia Reinhardt, but despite his love for her, he would remain married to Elsa until her death in 1945. Three years later he invited Reinhardt to come to America, and she did, settling in Santa Monica. After the conductor's death, she returned to Europe, settling in Switzerland, where she lived until her death in 1974.

After Munich, Bruno Walter was appointed chief conductor of the German wing at London's Covent Garden Opera and became music director of the German State Opera. In 1925 he began his involvement with the Salzburg Festival, organized in the early 1920s by the composer Richard Strauss, the poet and Strauss librettist Hugo von Hofmannsthal, and the producer/director Max Reinhardt, whom the conductor would encounter years later in Los Angeles.

In 1936 he was appointed music director of the Vienna State Opera, but it was to be a short tenure. Despite being Jewish, and thus a clear target for the Nazis, he put music first, even if it was seen as a provocative act. In June of 1936 he received death threats for engaging the African-American contralto Marian Anderson as the soloist in a performance of Brahms's *Alto Rhapsody*, and later that month Austrian Nazis threw stink bombs into the auditorium during a Walter-led performance of Wagner's *Tristan und Isolde*. Uprooted by the Anschluss in March 1938, he was offered French citizenship (which he accepted), but elected to move first to Lugano, Switzerland, and then settled permanently in Los Angeles after it had become clear that if he remained in neutral Switzerland, his opportunities for work would be nil.

On August 18 of that year, there occurred what the conductor later described as the greatest tragedy of his life. His daughter Gretel, romantically involved with the great basso Ezio Pinza, was shot and killed by her husband Robert Neppach, a German filmmaker. Although much of the story remains cloudy, it is known that Gretel began seeing Pinza in Salzburg, where Bruno Walter first conducted the singer in a celebrated performance of *Don Giovanni* in 1934 (after retiring from the Metropolitan Opera in 1948, Pinza would go on to star with Mary Martin on Broadway in *South Pacific* the next year and in 1954 in *Fanny*).

After stopping off to visit with Arturo Toscanini near Lucerne, Switzerland (Toscanini and Walter were both conducting at Salzburg then), Gretel had returned to her husband in Zurich. The next day Toscanini's daughter, Wally, called Pinza and told him that Neppach had shot her while she slept and then turned the gun on himself. Pinza immediately drove to Zurich, where he attended the funeral, during which Walter played the first movement of Beethoven's *Moonlight*

*Sonata.* "The next day I drove the Walters to their home in Lugano," Pinza later recalled. "The urn with Gretel's ashes in my car, the man I had grown to love as a father sitting beside me, silent with grief."

Two and a half months after Gretel was laid to rest in Lugano, the conductor, accompanied by Elsa and Lotte, sailed for America, settling in a bungalow at 608 Bedford Drive in Beverly Hills the following year. Back in California, Walter took up his friendships with old friends, including the writer Thomas Mann. In 1943 Gustav Mahler's widow, Alma, and her husband, Franz Werfel, moved next door. After Franz Werfel's and Elsa Walter's deaths in 1945, Hollywood gossip columnist Hedda Hopper wrote that Alma would marry Bruno Walter; Alma was furious, but Walter thought it wasn't such a bad idea.

During the ensuing years, Bruno Walter conducted extensively in America with the Chicago Symphony, Toscanini's NBC Symphony Orchestra, the Philadelphia Orchestra, and the Los Angeles Philharmonic, which, with the advent of Walter's compatriot Otto Klemperer in 1933, had evolved into national importance. From 1941 until 1959, he also conducted at the Metropolitan Opera and, after the war, made many return visits to Europe, returning to his former podiums in Salzburg, Munich, and Vienna, and helping launch the Edinburgh Festival.

During Bruno Walter's later life, he was engaged in making a series of stereo recordings with the Columbia Symphony Orchestra. His last concert appearance was as the conductor of the Los Angeles Philharmonic on December 4, 1960, with Van Cliburn as soloist.

Bruno Walter died of a heart attack at his Beverly Hills home February 16, 1962. He had converted to Catholicism, and his ashes were placed in a Catholic cemetery in Montagnola, Switzerland, not far from the grave of the Nobel laureate writer Herman Hesse (*Steppenwolf*), who had moved to the small village in the Italian-speaking section of the country in 1919.

• • • • • • •

Few classical conductors have lived as dramatic a life as Otto Klemperer. Once musical director of the Los Angeles Philharmonic Orchestra, he was later blacklisted by most U.S. orchestras for his erratic behavior, which on one occasion caused him to be beaten and left in a gutter. After he was found in a fleabag hotel in New York in 1954, his career was resurrected; within a few years, he had become a musical legend.

Like Bruno Walter, the now legendary conductor Otto Klemperer also had a daughter named Lotte. Both were Jewish; both were linked to provincial Breslau, Germany, where Klemperer was born on May 14, 1885; and both focused their talents on the core German repertoire, championing Mahler's then relatively unfamiliar music. Both enjoyed distinguished recording careers in later life as well.

But that is where any comparison essentially ends. Klemperer, unlike Walter, actually changed musical matters in the City of Angels, transforming in a decade a once adequate though provincial symphony orchestra into one that, at the least, was snapping at the heels of the reputations of America's best. And, unlike Walter (as well as many of the refugees), he—or at least his name—became identified with the city's main industry; his son, Werner, became well-known as a character actor worked successfully in film and television, although hardly in the way one would suppose the son of a man persecuted by the Nazis would hope. His most famous role was that of a bumbling Nazi prison camp boss in CBS's long-running *Hogan's Heroes* series. In his defense, it must be said that there are those who feel his portrayal of a Nazi officer as a fool was his way of insulting Hitler's military, for whom appearances counted for much.

Otto Klemperer's move to Los Angeles came about almost accidentally. In early 1933 Klemperer left Germany for Switzerland. "In the train from Berlin to Basle, there were almost only Jews," he recalled in a conversation with Peter Heyworth in 1973. "I had the feeling I would be arrested at the frontier, and the Jews as they crossed the Red Sea couldn't have been any happier than I was when I found myself on Swiss soil and free. Fourteen days later my wife came with the children and brought—oh miracle—money! Which she had baked into a cake. Two weeks later came our housekeeper, who had packed up our flat in Berlin, so we were all together.

"In the course of the summer [of 1933], I traveled to Rome to see Pacelli [Pope Pius XII] and ask for his help for the Jews," Klemperer also recalled. "Later that summer I met an American woman in

Florence who said, 'I hear that you have some trouble in Germany. Would you like to come to Los Angeles? We need a new conductor.' That was wonderful, so I said, 'Of course.'

"... there was a long conversation about salary," Klemperer recalled. "I thought it was too small, and [my agent] said L.A. couldn't pay more. Then I agreed, and after some concerts in Vienna and Salzburg in October 1933, I went to America. I was very glad to have this position because the winter was taken care of." Actually, it would be more than the winter that was taken care of. . . . Klemperer would remain with the Los Angeles Philharmonic for six years, becoming a U.S. citizen in 1937.

Gottfried Reinhardt, son of the German director-producer Max Reinhardt, later recalled Klemperer's introduction to Los Angeles's musical tradition; it happened after Klemperer's first concert with the orchestra, which Reinhardt attended with Salka Viertel, Charlie Chaplin, and the director King Vidor. After the concert, the trio visited the conductor in his dressing room, and as they were chatting, suddenly they heard Sousa's *Stars and Stripes* march. "What on earth is that?" Klemperer asked, according to Reinhardt. Klemperer stalked out of the dressing room and over to the stage where William Andrews Clark, Jr., a multimillionaire businessman, amateur musician, and president of the Philharmonic Association who originally endowed the organization in 1919, was conducting the march to a then empty hall. "Stop, stop at once!" Klemperer said, feeling that a temple dedicated to the arts was being desecrated. "But I always do this," Clark said meekly. "It's my hobby." And it was, indeed, his motive for subsidizing the orchestra, Reinhardt explained, adding that Klemperer's response was "Not while I'm here."

"I conducted every two weeks and the concerts were very well attended," Klemperer said of the orchestra that he described as "good. Not as good as the Boston or Philadelphia [orchestras] but very good. I was able to do newer works, Bruckner, Mahler and also Stravinsky. All that was new to Los Angeles. Little of Schoenberg's music though . . ." Klemperer felt the music of his compatriot Arnold Schoenberg, the inventor of the twelve-tone music system who had moved to Los Angeles in 1934, was too advanced for the audience, but on Klemperer's recommendation, Schoenberg would soon receive a teaching position at UCLA

Klemperer knew he wanted to be a conductor, as well as a composer, from an early age (he would later write an opera, several string quartets, and six symphonies in a lush, Mahlerian style). After first studying in Frankfurt, he moved on to Berlin, where he continued his studies, making his "official" conducting debut in 1906 leading Max Reinhardt's production of Offenbach's *Orpheus in Hades* at the Neues Theater (the previous year he actually made his debut—unseen—conducting the offstage orchestra in a performance of Mahler's Symphony No. 2 (the "Resurrection Symphony"). It was then that he first met Mahler, who would recommend him as the chorus director, and later conductor, of the Deutsches Landestheater in Prague. Further appointments over the next two decades included Hamburg, Strasbourg, Cologne, and Wiesbaden.

In 1927 Klemperer was appointed director of a branch of the Berlin State Opera chartered to perform new and recent works, as well as to present music from standard repertory nontraditionally. There, to audiences deliberately drawn in most part from factory and office workers, among the many landmark productions that make him the hero of musical modernists, he presented Stravinsky's *Oedipus Rex*, Schoenberg's *Ewartung*, Hindemith's *Cardillac,* and Janáček's *The House of the Dead*. After the project ended, he conducted at the State Opera, where on the fiftieth anniversary of Richard Wagner's death, he led a gala performance of *Tannhauser* shortly before he fled the country.

His tenure with the Los Angeles Philharmonic ended in 1939, about the time he had surgery to remove a tumor on his brain, reportedly resulting from a fall into a Berlin orchestra pit (there were stories that Nazi hooligans pushed him off the podium). Afterward Klemperer was partially paralyzed, and his longtime bipolar condition became more evident. His condition also brought on other serious problems, but due to the devoted attention of first his wife, Johanna, and later his only daughter, Lotte, he managed to keep conducting until 1971. According to musical historian Norman Lebrecht, he could not have continued his career (which would gain near legendary status through many recordings in the 1950s and '60s) without Lotte.

Because of Klemperer's severe bipolar disorder, in his worst moments his behavior could be highly embarrassing. In his depressive times, the condition brought him close to suicide. When he was on a "high," Lebrecht said, "he was beset by satyriasis, recklessly pursuing every woman within an arm's reach."

Lebrecht recalled a particularly telling event in Los Angeles. "Gustav Mahler's daughter, Anna, once found herself chased by him around a dining table." (Anna, then a well-known sculptor, was also the daughter of Klemperer's California neighbor, the composer's widow Alma Mahler Werfel. Her bronze bust of Klemperer stands in the foyer of the Dorothy Chandler Pavilion in Los Angeles.) "Knowing that Klemperer had been close to her parents, she breathlessly sought to preserve dignity and friendship," Lebrecht added. "'Dr. Klemperer,' she gasped, 'in Bach's B-minor mass, rehearsal figure 46, is that top note F or F-sharp?' Klemperer stopped as if stunned and delivered a magisterial analysis of the work. Music was the only interest that could override his furious compulsions."

Before Lotte looked after him, it was the lot of his wife, Johanna, a former soprano, to be first responsible for and then most humiliated by his condition. After the surgery Johanna wanted to have Klemperer, his tongue atrophied and one side of his face paralyzed, committed to a mental institution. He would have none of it; instead, he walked out on his family, saying he needed a year of freedom. Accompanied by the wife of the conductor Maurice Abramavel, he then proceeded to leave trail of unpaid bills across the country.

One day after he was reported missing in a front-page story in the *New York Times*, the paper printed a photograph of him behind bars. Released on bail, he was greeted by a crowd of reporters; the seventeen-year-old Lotte acting as an interpreter.

Most American orchestras immediately wrote him off their books, especially after a concert in Los Angeles when he wandered away and was found beaten up in a gutter. On his return to California after a European concert tour, he was blacklisted within his profession and denied a new passport. In 1954 an agent found him (via Lotte, with whom the agent was having a love affair) broke and living in a fleabag hotel in New York. When the agent asked Klemperer if he would accept a contract to conduct the Portland, Oregon, orchestra, the conductor initially refused—three thousand miles was too far to travel for a single gig. Lotte, however, convinced him, and both his and the agent's careers took a turn as dramatic as any of the plot twists in the operas Klemperer had famously conducted.

It was Beethoven—specifically his Seventh Symphony—that did it. Portland had never heard anything as heroic. The agent, Ronald Wilford, would become the most powerful force in classical music (he would much later be blamed for much of classical music's problems these days in Norman Lebrecht's *Who Killed Classical Music?*). Wilford also managed to get Klemperer's passport restored, after which the conductor flew to London, where in 1955 when Klemperer was seventy, the producer Walter Legge asked him to become the conductor of the Philharmonia Orchestra. (Legge had started the orchestra earlier to support EMI Classics recordings, and today it remains one of the finest in Britain.)

The results were startling. In a country hitherto not especially noted for orchestral excellence, Klemperer embarked on a series of concerts and recordings that demonstrated both his unmatched sense of a work's architectural integrity and its greatest—albeit usually heroic—potential. At the end of Klemperer's inaugural Beethoven cycle, one that stood the city on its ears, the London County Council commissioned a bust of Klemperer by Jacob Epstein that still stands in the Royal Festival Hall. In 1962 Klemperer made his Covent Garden Opera House debut with a performance of Beethoven's *Fidelio* (a recording with much the same cast has been recognized from its release as an unmatchable classic).

Even with his newfound fame, Klemperer continued to be accident prone, once suffering near fatal burns when his pipe caught fire in bed and he tried to put it out with whiskey. Also in bed he continued to be incorrigible. One morning in London when Lotte brought the then old man his breakfast tray, she found him in bed with a young woman. "This is my daughter, Lotte," he said to his companion. "And what did you say your name was?"

Otto Klemperer died on July 6, 1973, in Zurich, where he was buried in the city's Jewish cemetery.

Walt Disney (left) with Igor Stravinsky. Stravinsky, who categorized Disney's use of music from his *Rite of Spring* ballet as "an unresisting imbecility," nevertheless later sold the rights of additional music scores to the filmmaker.

# 11

## Russia in Hollywood

### *Igor Stravinsky*

Despite the fact that the talent gathered in Los Angeles during the 1930s and '40s made it, arguably, the cultural capital of America for a time, many—especially New Yorkers—considered the place a cultureless hick town (many, of course, still do). In fact, at least one New York critic claimed that after Igor Stravinsky and Arnold Schoenberg moved to Hollywood (Stravinsky in 1940, Schoenberg in 1934), their music was corrupted by the dollar. Schoenberg, the high priest of atonal music, "began to write tonal music again," wrote a New York critic, "and Stravinsky was reduced to writing music for Broadway revues and circus elephants (1942's *Circus Polka*) and standing by while Disney and [the conductor Leopold] Stokowski turned *The Rite of Spring* into a Jurassic theme park in *Fantasia*."

True, Stravinsky did write ballet music for Cole Porter's 1944 Broadway musical *Seven Lively Arts*, and his landmark ballet, premiered in Paris in 1913, was used in *Fantasia*, Disney's still popular 1940 film that combined animation and classical music (most notoriously, perhaps, with a ballet corps of hippos dancing to *The Dance of the Hours* from Ponchielli's opera *La Gioconda*). And Schoenberg did write some tonal music, including his haunting Piano Concerto.

If Stravinsky sold out to commercial Hollywood, he did it because he couldn't turn down the money, but he also continued to write "serious" music, most notably his 1945 Symphony in Three Movements (its second movement, with its prominent harp solo, was originally intended to accompany the vision of the Virgin Mary in the movie adaptation of his fellow refugee Franz Werfel's book *The Song of Bernadette*—Alfred Newman ended up scoring the movie and won an Oscar for his work), the 1948 ballet *Orpheus*, and 1946's *Ebony Concerto*, composed for clarinetist Woody Herman.

Arnold Schoenberg's tonal music was no less serious—to him, anyway—than his atonal music. In any event, after composing the tone-based Piano Concerto and String Trio, Schoenberg returned to his twelve-tone atonal style for his Fourth String Quartet.

The point is that although both composers may have been affected by the dollar (Schoenberg, especially, needed money all of his life), despite some odd leaps (Stravinsky followed his *Ebony Concerto* with a neo-medieval Mass), both men turned out some of their best music while in Hollywood.

Igor Stravinsky was born at Oranienbaum on the Gulf of Finland on June 5, 1882. He was raised in nearby Saint Petersburg, where his father was a leading bass at the Mariinsky Theater. Pressured by his father, he originally studied to be a lawyer until at the age of twenty, in 1902, he decided he wanted to be a composer and visited the famous musician Nicolai Rimsky-Korsakov to seek career advice. After he played some of his early compositions for the man who was his hero, Rimsky told him, "Don't quit law school."

Despite his doubts, however, the older musician suggested that if Stravinsky wanted to try for a successful career in music, he could take classes in harmony and counterpoint from one of his assistants. Three years later Rimsky took Stravinsky on as a private pupil, a collaboration that, until 1908, exposed the younger man to the older composer's consummate mastery of orchestration, as well as his abiding love of the folktales and tunes of Mother Russia.

That he learned well was soon proven. In February of 1909, Stravinsky wrote a short, jubilant piece called *Fireworks* in celebration of the marriage of his mentor's daughter; it lead directly to the composition of the piece that brought the composer his first taste of international fame. In the audience for that first performance of *Fireworks* was Serge Diaghilev, the impresario of the newly formed Ballets Russes, who loved what he heard. After testing Stravinsky's talent by assigning him to orchestrate music by Chopin for use by the ballet, Diaghilev cabled him to compose a huge original ballet: *The Firebird*. When it premiered in Paris on June 25, 1910, to a tremendous ovation and press reviews, the twenty-eight-year-old composer was instantly the toast of the town and, as soon as the piece made the rounds, of other world capitals as well (years later he would often conduct the piece at the Hollywood Bowl). With *The Firebird*, Stravinsky was then hailed—and is still remembered—as the creator of the first modern ballet and a talent who would change the face of contemporary music. He did all this—and more.

It began quickly. During his stay in Paris after the premiere of his ballet, Stravinsky composed two more major works for the Ballets Russes. Along with *The Firebird*, the two new ballets, *Petrushka* (composed in 1911) and *The Rite of Spring,* would endure as landmarks of twentieth-century music. The savagely dissonant *The Rite of Spring*, presented with choreography by the famous dancer Vaslav Nijinsky, caused a riot at its May 1913 premiere in Paris's Théâtre des Champs-Elysées.

World War I caused Stravinsky to seek refuge in Switzerland and, apparently, reassess his roots. Although he was not to return to his homeland until 1962, his wartime works are almost exclusively concerned with Russian folktales and songs. They include 1918's very popular short play *L'Histoire du Soldat (A Soldier's Tale)*, with spoken narration and instrumental music; the fable *Renard*, performed with song and dance, which was composed in 1916 but not performed until 1922; and 1923's choral ballet *Les Noces (The Wedding)*.

The unique combination of instruments of distinct timbres of *A Soldier's Tale*—clarinet, bassoon, tenor and bass trombones, double bass, cornet, violin, and percussion—would become almost a cliché among modern composers a generation later. Another notable innovation of orchestral technique that can be partially attributed to Stravinsky is the exploitation of the extreme ranges of instruments. The most famous passage in this regard is the opening of *The Rite of Spring,* where Stravinsky uses the ultimate reaches of the bassoon to simulate the symbolic "awakening" of a spring morning. Despite his later criticism of the use of music from *The Rite of Spring* in *Fantasia* as "an unresisting imbecility," Stravinsky also sold options to the scores of *Renard* and *The Firebird* to Disney. Such has always been the lure of Hollywood's checkbook culture.

Returning to Paris after World War I, Stravinsky became part of the city's soon thriving cultural life and collaborated with several of the century's most famous talents. In addition to reuniting with Diaghilev and his Ballets Russes, he collaborated with Pablo Picasso on the 1920 ballet *Pulcinella* (based on music by the eighteenth-century composer Pergolesi, the piece opened a long period of neoclassicism in Stravinsky's music), with Jean Cocteau on *Oedipus Rex* (1927), and with George Balanchine, future founder of the New York City Ballet, on the following year's *Apollon Musagete.* He also wrote several works to help him earn his living as a pianist, among them his Piano Concerto.

Unlike many composers, at least during the 1920s, Stravinsky seems to have been as talented at finding patrons to support him and his family as he was at writing music (an early, anonymous patron was the composer Leopold Stokowski). One reason was his ability to ingratiate himself with the musical establishment and his frequent concertizing in such capitals as London, New York, Berlin, and, of course, Paris.

In 1906 he married his cousin Katerina Nossenko, and the union would last for thirty-three years until her death in 1939. That, however, didn't stop Stravinsky from having many extramarital affairs, including one with Coco Chanel and a longtime one with the lady he would marry in 1940 in New York, where the pair had fled from Nazi-occupied France: Vera de Bosset.

Five years earlier Stravinsky had visited Hollywood, and his memory of the money being made by composers in the film capital clearly influenced the couple to soon move there. "It's a very interesting place," he told an Italian newspaper in a June 1935 interview following his first visit to the film capital. "I visited several studios, each of which is a kind of principality with its own borders, trenches, police cannons, [and] machine guns, as well as its ministers for the voracious technical and artistic operations. At Metro Goldwyn Mayer I saw forty salaried composers all working from morning to night to produce music. This way, the directors avoid reruns of music that already exists and do not have to pay royalties to other composers.

"I wanted to meet the head of the company, Mr. Mayer, and an interview was arranged. I was led through a gray corridor to a gray room crowded with others waiting like myself. I remained there a long time during which everyone talked about Mr. Mayer though no one had seen him and he may have well have been a myth. But at long last a door opened and a little man with a large beak appeared, followed by two lieutenants. He approached me, nodded, and said: 'I am a man like others with a lot to do.' And with this, he shook my hand and left. At least I can testify Mr. Mayer is not a myth."

Perhaps Stravinsky should have remembered his earlier impression more carefully before moving to Hollywood. Not only would he be frustrated by the Hollywood "system," but as it turned out, his music was wrong for the place, nothing like that being turned out daily by those "forty salaried composers" he saw working at MGM or by fellow émigrés and refugees like Erich Korngold. Although he worked fairly diligently at it, Stravinsky, despite being offered several film projects, would never compose a successful movie score, except more or less by default with *Fantasia.*

He was certainly famous enough, more so than just about any of his fellow refugees. In fact, as author Lawrence Wechsler relates, when George Gershwin decided that the only way he could prove the legitimacy of his music was to compose a string quartet (in 1929 he had composed a Lullaby for String Quartet), he approached the famous émigré and refugee composers in Southern California, asking them if they would show him how to do it.

The story goes that one day Gershwin wrote Stravinsky promising to pay him any fee he felt appropriate if he would teach him how to compose the piece. Stravinsky asked Gershwin how much money he made a year, and after Gershwin told him, Stravinsky replied by return mail, "In that case won't you please take *me* on as *your* student?"

The reason for Stravinsky's failure in the film industry is not hard to understand . . . simply listen to his scores of the late 1930s and early 1940s. Hollywood cinema of the period demanded grand continuity (like Korngold's lush symphonic tone poems). Stravinsky's music, with its patterned discontinuities, was much better suited to dancing.

One of the proudest achievements of Stravinsky's Hollywood years was his opera *The Rake's Progress*, completed in 1951 and premiered by the Metropolitan Opera in 1953. Written to a libretto by W. H. Auden and Chester Kallman (Auden's life partner) and based on the etchings of William Hogarth of eighteenth-century London, the opera is a culmination of Stravinsky's neoclassical style begun a generation earlier. The music was controversial from the start; within the classical harmonies echoing the operas of Mozart, Gluck, and Monteverdi, Stravinsky interjects startling dissonances. The piece also features the composer's now trademarked off-rhythms, which along with his discontinuities, were at the root of his problem writing film music.

In any event, after *The Rake's Progress*, Stravinsky ended his experiments in neoclassicism and began composing in the atonal twelve-tone system invented by the recently deceased Arnold Schoenberg as he reinterpreted it. Possibly the reason for this change was that his opera was heavily criticized for being too backward looking, even by critics who had earlier applauded his innovation. Another reason for his conversion to the twelve-tone system—also known as "serial music" because of its ordering of pitches—was the presence of a conductor and musicologist named Robert Craft, then twenty-three years old, who urged the composer to, in his words, "jump on the twelve-tone bandwagon." In any event, atonality would largely define Stravinsky's style until his death.

Craft also served another need. After arriving in Hollywood, Stravinsky and Vera, like most of the other refugees, associated largely with people they felt most comfortable with, in their case a ring of Russian friends and contacts (Los Angeles still boasts a huge Russian population). But when he decided to write an opera with Auden and Kallman, he realized he needed to be involved more with the English-speaking world, a decision that also coincided with his meeting Craft, who would live with the composer and his wife until Stravinsky's death. During those years he would be Stravinsky's door to the English language and culture, advisor, chronicler, assistant conductor, and general factotum for both musical and social tasks.

Stravinsky started using the new style cautiously in small works like 1952's *Cantata on Medieval English Verses* and 1954's *In Memoriam Dylan Thomas*. As his confidence grew, he expanded into larger works, often based on the Bible, like *Threni* (1958) and *The Flood* (1962). An important transitional work of this period was Stravinsky's return to ballet, *Agon*, a work for twelve dancers written between 1954 and 1957 that utilizes both his neoclassic style, as well as his interpretation of serialism. The ballet is, in fact, a sort of miniature encyclopedia of Stravinsky, containing many of the signatures to be found throughout his compositions.

In 1962 Stravinsky accepted an invitation to return to Russia for a series of concerts, but he remained firmly based in the West. The Stravinskys moved to New York in 1969 (when asked why he would uproot himself so late in life, he replied, "So I can mutate faster"). It was there that he died on April 6, 1971, at the age of eighty-nine. He was buried in Venice, Italy, on the cemetery island of San Michele, near the grave of his first major patron, Serge Diaghilev. Today there are few reminders of his years in Hollywood—his home at 1260 Weatherly Drive in Beverly Hills is still there, and he is honored by a star on the Hollywood Walk of Fame at 6340 Hollywood Boulevard.

What does remain is all the music he composed under Los Angeles's palm trees. Taking many compositional styles, he transformed them into something unmistakably his own. That is his legacy.

Vera died in 1983 and was buried next to her husband.

The legendary violinist Jascha Heifetz onstage circa 1940. One of the most famous musicians in the world in the 1930s and '40s, he would die lonely and virtually forgotten.

# 12
.......

# The Reclusive Violin Genius

## *Jascha Heifetz*

**M**any of the refugees and émigrés in this book wrote music for the movies or toiled away writing books or scripts for films. But not many of them—except for the actors, actresses, and directors who moved to Hollywood especially to make movies like Marlene Dietrich, Greta Garbo, David Niven, and Alfred Hitchcock—actually starred *as themselves* in films.

One major exception was the émigré Jascha Heifetz, still considered by many the greatest violinist of the twentieth century. That is certainly how the world thought of him between the wars, when classical music was far more mainstream than it is today. As with countless other examples, when the mavens of Hollywood smelled a good thing, they went after it. In 1939 Sam Goldwyn, anxious to cash in on the fame of this classical superstar, decided to cobble together a showcase for him; the film *They Shall Have Music* was the result, made soon after Heifetz completed his twentieth U.S. concert tour.

Our culture has changed so much since 1939 that it is difficult to even imagine that a story line like that of *They Shall Have Music* would be greenlighted. The plot is simple—and simplistic. A street kid—turned youthful criminal—runs away from home and is taken in by a music school. When the music school hits hard times, he takes it on himself to ask the famous violinist to play a benefit to save the place. Frankie—the kid's name—was played by Gene Reynolds, who went on to become a film director; among his credits are several episodes of TV's *M.A.S.H.* Starring in a cast that was a virtual "who's who" of character actors of the time (among them Walter Brennan and Marjorie Main) was Joel McCrea, who would go on to become one of Hollywood's great western actors, starring in the iconic *The Virginian* seven years later. In 1947 Heifetz would again appear in a film, *Carnegie Hall*, but as a performer, not a plot character.

Heifetz was not a refugee from Nazism, but from the Russian Revolution, which he fled by making his way through Siberia and the Orient when he was sixteen (or, more likely, eighteen—Heifetz gave both 1899 and 1901 as his birth date; most authorities agree on the earlier date). After making his American concert debut at Carnegie Hall on October 27, 1917, he was barraged by concert offers and exactly ten days later made his first recordings for RCA Victor, with which he would be associated for his entire career.

No wonder. Of the debut, the noted critic Samuel Chotzinoff reported, "The 16-year-old violinist seemed the most unconcerned of all the people in the hall as he walked out on the stage and proceeded to give an exhibition of such extraordinary virtuosity and musicianship as had not previously been heard in that historic auditorium." Overnight, Jascha Heifetz became the musical idol of America, and during that first year he made thirty appearances in New York alone.

Jascha was born in Vilnius, Lithuania, then known as Vilna and part of Russia, to Ruvin and Anna Heifetz, a professional pianist. His father was concertmaster of the Vilna Symphony Orchestra, and although it is not uncommon for children of musicians to become musicians themselves, there clearly was something very special about young Jascha. He began playing a quarter-sized violin at the age of three, and by the time he was seven, he played his first public concert in Kovno, Lithuania, performing Mendelssohn's difficult, virtuosic Violin Concerto.

In 1910 the eleven-year-old prodigy entered the St. Petersburg Conservatory and soon became a private student of Leopold Auer, a famous Hungarian violin teacher to whom Tchaikovsky dedicated his Violin Concerto (Auer, whose famous students would also include Nathan Milstein and Efrem Zimbalist, would follow Heifetz to America the year after his former student arrived. He ended his career on the faculty of Philadelphia's Curtis Institute of Music).

By the age of twelve, the young violinist was touring extensively in Scandanavia and Germany. In Berlin he would meet the legendary Fritz Kreisler, who famously said of Heifetz's talent: "Now we can all break our fiddles across our knees."

"You know," Heifetz later said of those years, "'child prodigism'— if I may coin a word—is a disease which is generally fatal. I was among the few to have the good fortune to survive. But I had the advantage of a great teacher in Professor Auer, and a family that instinctively had a high regard for music, very good taste and a horror of mediocrity."

His American debut and recording contract were followed by a triumphant tour of the United States and the beginnings of worldwide fame. He made his first London appearance on May 5, 1920, toured Australia (1921), the Orient (1923), Palestine (1926), and South America. In 1934 he revisited Russia, where he was welcomed enthusiastically. Heifetz became a naturalized American citizen in 1925, and in the 1940s settled into a mansion atop one of the Beverly Hills in California, where he built a studio and lived until his death.

Throughout his life, Heifetz was known for his flawless technical style. But he was also accused of sounding formal and mechanical, which was also reflected in his austere personality. But the fierce virtuosity never faltered, even into his seventies, and he ended up recording more than eighty albums in his lifetime. Under the pseudonym Jim Hoyl, he even wrote a pop song called *When You Make Love to Me (Don't Make Believe)*, sung by Margaret Whiting.

When Heifetz reached his sixties, after half a century of concertizing, he began to gradually curtail his appearances and gave his last public recital in 1972. For a decade following 1962, he taught classes for exceptionally talented pupils at the University of Southern California in Los Angeles. In 1974 he made his last public appearance and thereby brought to a close one of the most extraordinary violin careers in history. Included among his manifold honors was the French Legion of Honor, a recognition of the many charity recitals he performed in France. Heifetz also received many Grammy Awards, including the elusive Lifetime Achievement Award in 1989, and was posthumously inducted into the Grammy Hall of Fame in 1999.

Many celebrities live very private lives, but Heifetz was almost manic about isolating himself from the public. There is very little known about his offstage life other than that he was married twice, and that, apparently, is how he wanted it. In 1939, according to an article by Tim Page in *The New Criterion*, he summed up his life for the musicologist Deems Taylor: "Born in Russia, first lessons at three, debut in Russia at seven, debut in America in 1917. That's all there is to say, really. About two lines."

We know from firsthand reports that he handled his students with steel-rod control, seemingly little tempered with humor. Discipline was high on the list values Heifetz demanded of his students ("It's something you have to do, so you might as well do it and get it over with," he said often).

But, apparently, there was more. The Indonesian-born violinist Ayke Agus, who had grown up listening to his records, was one of his students at U.S.C. She is also one of the few people who have tried to write a biography of this reclusive, private man, based on a fifteen-year relationship that began in 1971 when she entered his class and lasted until his death. Because Agus was a talented pianist, as well as a violinist, he made her the class accompanist. But it wasn't long before she became his personal accompanist and, as he aged, his indispensable companion. Anne-Marie Bigot de Cornuel, a celebrated seventeenth-century Parisian hostess, once said, "No man is a hero to his valet." In this case it was not a valet but the accompanist who wrote the "tell all" book.

Agus's book, *Heifetz As I Knew Him*, portrays the famous violinist in his later years as controlling, manipulative, tyrannical, sadistic, inflexible, narrow-minded, suspicious, reclusive, and as his health declined, increasingly erratic, unpredictable, and irrational. When Agus met him, he was retiring from the stage, but still played chamber music privately with friends and students, and he did not stop playing for himself until almost the end.

It is naturally Agus's personal relationship with Heifetz that is central to her portrait. Apparently, the violinist added musical and domestic duties to her services until Agus claims she spent virtually all her time at his beck and call, finally doing everything for him, from running his household to administering his eyedrops. She claims it was entirely due to her coaxing and assistance that he resumed work on his unfinished transcriptions. Agus, a prodigy of sorts, concludes that, like her, Heifetz was exploited by his parents, but unlike her, he was spoiled by them as well, making him "a superannuated, insecure, and immature child," craving but alienating friends and relationships with sudden mood swings, cruel practical jokes, and unkind remarks.

In her book, she discreetly avoids discussing his marital and family life—the facts about that, insofar as they can be discovered, tend to support Agus's observations, self-serving as critics have found them. Virtually nothing is known about his marriages other than that they ended in nasty divorces.

His first wife was Florence Vidor, a silent-screen star who divorced the great director King Vidor in 1925 but kept her married name for acting purposes. She was one of many silent actors who failed to make the transition to sound. Her last silent films had talking sequences added to them to make them commercially viable, and in her last film, 1929's *Chinatown Nights*, her voice was dubbed by another actress. Disillusioned with the direction of her career, she married Heifetz in 1928 and, following the release of *Chinatown Nights*, quit the industry.

The couple had two children before their 1946 divorce. Florence died of heart failure in Pacific Palisades, California, on November 3, 1977.

As he got older, Heifetz became profoundly depressed. He underwent a serious shoulder operation and suffered many increasingly dangerous falls. An intensely private person, he lived alone even when his health was failing, and Agus took it upon herself—or was asked—to cope with all his problems. Even after her marriage, she continued to run his household and attend to his needs.

On his fourth tour to Israel in 1953, Heifetz included in his recitals the Violin Sonata by Richard Strauss. Strauss was considered a Nazi composer, and his works were unofficially banned in Israel, along with those of Richard Wagner. Despite the fact that the Holocaust was fresh in everyone's memory and a plea from the Israeli minister of education, Heifetz didn't change a thing, affirming that "the music is above these factors . . . I will not change my program. I have the right to decide on my repertoire." Nevertheless, throughout his tour the performance of the Strauss sonata was followed by dead silence and no applause.

Some reacted more violently. After his recital in Jerusalem, he was attacked and struck on his right arm with an iron bar by a man outside his hotel. As the attacker fled, Heifetz shouted to the friends who were with him (some of whom were armed), "Shoot that man, he tried to kill me." But the assailant escaped and was never found.

The incident made headlines around the world, and Heifetz defiantly announced that he would not stop playing Strauss. As more and more threats came, he decided to drop the Strauss sonata from his next recital without explanation. His last concert of the tour was canceled when his right arm began to hurt. He left Israel and did not return until 1970.

Not surprisingly, when he died on December 10, 1987, Heifetz was lonely and virtually forgotten. The music studio at his home (designed by Lloyd Wright, the son of Frank Lloyd Wright) lived on, however. After Heifetz died, his home was bought by the actor James Woods, who, as an alternative to tearing down the studio, called Los Angeles's Colburn School (which provides music, dance, and drama training) and asked if they wanted it. After the school raised the money to buy it, the studio was torn down and stored for a number of years before being installed in the present school seven years ago.

That studio—and of course, all those recordings—is about all that remains in Los Angeles to remind them that one of the world's greatest musicians once lived—and made music—there.

Sergei Rachmaninoff in a formal portrait. His romantic compositions proved to be a musical vein of gold, often mined by later film composers.

# 13
······

# Film Music

## *Sergei Rachmaninoff and Erich Korngold*

For two generations, the Garden of Allah, a hotel and bungalow complex built in 1918 by the famous silent-screen star Alla Nazimova (godmother, incidentally, to Nancy Reagan), was the apple in filmdom's Eden. Located on three and a half lushly landscaped acres where the streetcar line then ended, at the corner of Sunset Boulevard and Crescent Heights in what is now West Hollywood, it quickly became famous as a home for actors, film writers, musicians, and just plain eccentrics, many of whom lived there more or less permanently. One such tenant was Harpo Marx, the tousle-headed, mute member of the famous comedy group, who actually played the harp.

"My little bungalow in the Garden of Allah was a peaceful retreat," Marx recalled in his 1961 autobiography. "It was the best place to practice I ever had until a piano player moved into a bungalow across from mine and shattered the peace. When my new neighbor started to bang away, I couldn't hear anything below a *forte* on my harp," Marx continued. "The new guest was Sergei Rachmaninoff, and they (the management) were not about to ask him to move. I was flattered to have such a distinguished guest, but I still had to practice.

"So I got rid of him my own way," Marx added. "I opened the door and all the windows in my place and began to play the first four bars of [his] Prelude in C-sharp Minor, over and over, *fortissimo*. Two hours later my fingers were getting numb, but I didn't let up until I heard a thunderous crash of notes from across the way . . . like the keyboard had been attached to a pair of sledgehammers. Rachmaninoff [demanded] to be moved to another bungalow, the farthest from that dreadful harpist. And peace returned to the Garden."

As big a noise as he made in the Garden of Allah, Rachmaninoff was, as Harpo Marx acknowledged, making a gigantic noise in the music world of the era. And he had been doing so since the premiere of his Second Piano Concerto in Moscow in 1901. Throughout the golden age of Hollywood film, his lushly romantic music, like that of his older compatriot and acquaintance, Pyotr Il'yich Tchaikovsky, proved to be a vein of purest gold, perfect for mining by countless composers of film music.

Today his most familiar work—recently polled as Britain's most popular classical work (probably America's, too)—is that selfsame Piano Concerto No 2 (to give it its formal name). In 1945 music from the concerto swirled throughout the triple-Oscar-nominated, David Lean–directed British weeper *Brief Encounter*. That same year Frank Sinatra recorded a song written by Ted Mossman and Buddy Kaye to the hyper-romantic theme of the third movement of the concerto. Since then, to quote one observer, performances of the song, "Full Moon and Empty Arms," have been "unrelenting." "Rachh-maninoff?" Marilyn Monroe remarks to Tom Ewell in *The Seven-Year Itch* (1955). "The 'Second Piano Concerto,'" he explains. "It isn't fair," she says. "Not fair? Why?" "Every time I hear it I go to pieces." So, too, before and since, have millions.

It nearly didn't happen. Born the fifth child of a Russian aristocratic family on April 1, 1873, near Novgorod, Russia, the young Sergei had seen his father squander the family fortune and their estate near Novgorod auctioned off, his sister die in a diphtheria epidemic, and his parents separate, by the time he was twelve. Not surprisingly, he failed all his studies that year. To develop his pianistic talent, Rachmaninoff was shipped off to Moscow to live and study with a humorless disciplinarian, eventually to be replaced by the Moscow

Conservatory. People started noticing him, most importantly, Pyotr Il'yich Tchaikovsky, who was in the audience for the performances of Rachmaninoff's gold-medal-winning graduation piece, the opera *Aleko*. When Tchaikovsky died on November 6, 1893, the twenty-one-year-old Rachmaninoff composed his Elegiac Trio as a memorial.

In 1896 the young composer's First Symphony was premiered to devastating reviews (it didn't help that the concert's conductor, composer Alexander Glazunov, was drunk). Sergei was devastated and composed little during the following three years, living in a deep state of depression. Many commentators blame his later stoic personality on the experience.

As were his friends, Rachmaninoff was worried about his mental health and consulted many people about overcoming his composing block. Among them was Count Leo Tolstoy, who offered the somewhat less than helpful advice to keep trying. Finally the fledgling composer consulted a practitioner of the new science of psychology and recovered his self-esteem, which he attributed to hypnosis. Rachmaninoff began composing again (one of the first products of his cure was the Second Piano Concerto) and married his cousin Natalia, with whom he fathered two children.

In 1909 he composed his notoriously difficult Third Piano Concerto for a twenty-concert tour of the United States, playing it twice in New York, once under the baton of Gustav Mahler, then conductor of the New York Philharmonic. Following the Russian Revolution in 1917, he and his family briefly settled in Stockholm but soon moved to New York, where they bought a house on Riverside Drive and decorated it in a style that was later described as "Czarist Imperial."

Before moving to America, he had composed 135 works; afterward there would be only ten more. But that was all it took to establish him forever in the firmament of classical composers. That and the support he received from celebrated musicians like Vladimir Horowitz.

In 1942 Rachmaninoff, battling cancer, moved from New York to the warmer climate of Los Angeles on the advice of his doctors. After his short stay at the Garden of Allah, he and Natalia rented a large estate on Tower Road in Beverly Hills with a large garden, a swimming pool, and a huge music room that could hold two pianos. There the composer and Horowitz would often concertize for themselves and their friends.

On two memorable occasions they invited some four dozen friends for private duo-piano concerts. The first one, given on June 15, featured Mozart's two-piano Sonata K. 447 and Rachmaninoff's Symphonic Dances. One guest later reported that the audience was overcome by the power of the performance and the joy that each player clearly experienced, each fully aware of the other's greatness. "After the last note [of the Symphonic Dances] no one spoke," the guest added. "Time seemed to have stopped."

A highlight of the 1942 summer season at the Hollywood Bowl was the July appearance of Rachmaninoff playing the Second Piano Concerto. The following month Horowitz played the composer's Third Piano Concerto (August 7 and 8) with conductor William Steinberg. The gaunt, nearly pathologically shy composer attended the second of the two concerts, sitting in the last row of the huge amphitheater so no one would recognize him. When the performance ended, Rachmaninoff overcame his shyness enough to walk down the many steps of the Bowl and onto the stage. "This is the way I have always dreamed my concerto should be played but never expected to hear it that way on earth," he said. The audience of twenty-three thousand stood and applauded. Horowitz later said, "It was the greatest moment of my life."

Six months later, Rachmaninoff, who had for most of his later career maintained a fifty-concert-a-year tour schedule, left on a tour that opened on February 3, 1943, in State College, Pennsylvania. By the time he arrived in New Orleans for a concert date on February 22, he had become so ill that he decided to cancel the rest of the tour and return to Los Angeles to see a (Russian) doctor. Diagnosed as having melanoma, a rapidly spreading cancer that had already invaded his liver, lungs, and bones, he was given less than one month to live. His last words to his friend Vladimir Horowitz were "Good bye . . . I will not see you again."

On March 28, 1943, Sergei Rachmaninoff died and was buried in the Kensico Cemetery near New York City.

• • • • • • •

More than Rachmaninoff, more than just about anyone else, in fact, it would be the music of a thirty-seven-year-old émigré that became a stylistic common denominator of movie music in Hollywood's golden age, and its influence is still felt. Once described as an "apostle of romance, emotion, and beauty in music," Erich Wolfgang Korngold was already famed for his classical compositions. After settling permanently in Hollywood in 1938, he and the industry discovered he had a talent for writing film music in a heroic style that was perfect for such classic movies as 1938's *The Adventures of Robin Hood* and 1940's *The Sea Hawk*, both starring the era's swashbuckler *sans pareil*, Errol Flynn. He could also write music that was emotionally touching, as he did for the 1942 film starring Ronald Reagan, *King's Row*.

Other film composers—Alfred Newman for one—may have won more Oscars, but that was after music's tremendous importance in a film's success began to be realized. It was Korngold who showed the way, and showed it so memorably he has deservedly been called the father of modern film music. His brassy adventure themes and passionate romantic melodies are today hallmarks of film scores from John Williams's *Star Wars* trilogy to Howard Shore's multiple Oscar and Grammy–winning scores for *The Lord of the Rings* films.

And, like many of the sentimental movies of the time, Korngold's life, begun in glory, would have a bittersweet ending.

Born in Brno, Czechoslovakia, on May 29, 1897, to a frustrated composer turned music critic named Julius Korngold and his wife Josephine, in

Erich Korngold composing at his piano circa 1939. Much of modern film music, including such familiar scores as those for the *Star Wars* and *Raiders of the Lost Ark* series, was inspired by his film scores of the late 1930s and '40s.

his youth Erich was considered so remarkable a prodigy he was often compared to Wolfgang Amadeus Mozart. The composer/conductor Gustav Mahler was probably the first major musician to publicly acknowledge his talent, hailing the nine-year-old budding composer as "a genius." Four years later in 1911, after hearing an overture composed by Korngold, Richard Strauss, whose famous opera *Der Rosenkavalier* ("The Knight of the Rose") had just premiered, wrote young Erich's father, "Such mastery fills me with awe and fear."

Strauss, famous today for his symphonic tone poems such as *Also Sprach Zarathustra* (famously used in the opening of Stanley Kubrick's film *2001*) and *Don Quixote*, and for operas like *Der Rosenkavalier* and *Elektra*, clearly had an influence on Korngold, whose movie music has been likened to symphonic tone poems and opera without words. Giacomo Puccini, whose popular operas *La Bohème* and *Tosca* often have been mined for movie music, agreed: "[Korngold] has so much talent," he wrote, "he could easily give us half and still have enough left for himself."

At eleven, Korngold composed an instantly popular ballet score that was given its premiere in a command performance for Emperor Franz Josef at the Vienna Court Opera. Six years later his first two operas premiered as a double bill in Munich, cast with several of the greatest singers of the time and conducted by Gustav Mahler's protégé Bruno Walter, himself destined to become a legendary conductor and an émigré neighbor of Korngold in Los Angeles.

During the First World War, Korngold was drafted and appointed music director of his regiment, which allowed him to continue composing for the duration. Among the projects he was working on what would be his most famous opera, *Die Tote Stadt* (The Dead City). It was an immediate hit when it was premiered in Cologne in 1921 under the direction of Otto Klemperer, who a little more than a decade later would become the music director of the Los Angeles Philharmonic. The work soon entered the repertory of London's Covent Garden Opera House and the Metropolitan in New York.

During the next few years Korngold wrote another opera and several more serious pieces and arranged the first successful performing edition of "waltz king" Johann Strauss, Jr.,'s operetta *Eine Nacht in Venedig* ("One Night in Venice"). And by such seemingly insignificant things can people's lives be changed forever. Hollywood soon called, and his response almost certainly saved him and his family from death in a concentration camp.

It was all because of the legendary theater producer Max Reinhardt, who knowing what Korngold had done with the Strauss operetta, asked Korngold to collaborate on a 1929 production of the composer's popular *Die Fledermaus* ("The Bat"). Four years later Reinhardt would come to Los Angeles and stage Shakespeare's *A Midsummer Night's Dream* at the Hollywood Bowl—a production that is still remembered as one of the outstanding events of the Bowl's eighty-five-year history.

The following year, 1935, Reinhardt contacted Korngold to adapt Mendelssohn's famous *Midsummer Night's Dream* incidental music for the 114-minute film Warner Bros. made of the production. Korngold managed to do more than that. Once, when Arnold Schoenberg demanded control of the dialogue in MGM's production of Pearl Buck's *The Good Earth*, the studio's production chief, Irving Thalberg, more or less laughed him out of his office.

But that is exactly what Korngold got in parts of the *Midsummer Night's Dream* film. Victor Jory, who played Oberon in the movie, once recalled that Korngold carefully rehearsed him in the precise rhythms that he wanted for the famous speech that begins "I know a bank where the wild thyme grows. . . ." When it came to the actual filming, Korngold lay in some bushes out of camera range and literally conducted Jory's performance as though he was singing his lines. (William Dieterle, the film's director, was in full accord with Korngold's wishes.) While with Warner, Korngold also built up the studio's orchestra, which at the time sounded more like a glorified dance band than a proper symphony orchestra.

Although the film wasn't considered much of a success (despite winning two Oscars), Warner Bros. president Jack Warner believed Korngold had done more for movie music than anyone since sound was pioneered by the studio seven years earlier. As he also worked fast, a crucial talent in Hollywood, the studio offered him a one-year contract. Korngold turned it down, preferring for the time to freelance on the studio's *Captain Blood* (1935) and Paramount's *Give Us This Night*.

In the end, however, the composer signed a contract with Warner Bros. that not only paid him a lot of money, but allowed him first choice of any movie on the studio's schedule. His third score for them would be for the 1936 film *Anthony Adverse*, based on an epic best seller of the time, and the studio's most ambitious project. His score won the composer his first Oscar. (In between *Captain Blood* and *Anthony Adverse*, Korngold wrote and arranged the music for the all-black fantasy *Green Pastures* and was said to have loved working with the spirituals that comprised much of the score.)

Despite his recognition and high salary in Hollywood (as well as liking the weather), Vienna—and opera—still called. He had an opera ready—*Die Kathrin*—and a commitment from the Vienna State Opera to stage it. So, despite the looming Nazi threat, he and his family returned to Vienna in 1937. Luckily, reason prevailed. With German troops poised at the borders of Austria awaiting the order to annex the country, Korngold got his father and family out of the country with only days to spare. The score of *Die Kathrin*, as well as the scores of much of his other music, was smuggled out of Austria after being banned—like all music by Jewish composers.

Back in Hollywood, Korngold accepted a new contract from Warner Bros. (a new and highly unusual addition for its time specified that he would be credited on a separate frame in the film's titles and that his name would also appear in all advertising). His next film, *The Adventures of Robin Hood,* won him his second Oscar in 1938.

A close hearing of his music will quickly make apparent why Erich Korngold was so valued in the film capital. Take the music for 1940's

*The Sea Hawk*, a film about Elizabethan England's conflict with Spain and its Armada. Some critics attribute the rousing nature much of the music to Korngold's recognition of the contemporary British resistance to Hitler's pending invasion of Great Britain, thwarted by the heroism of young fighter pilots who fought the Luftwaffe to a standstill in the Battle of Britain. (Prime Minister Winston Churchill's homage to the outnumbered British Air Force—"Never in the field of human conquest has so much been owed by so many to so few"—provides a tangible indication of the emotional state of the times.) In the same film, Korngold's love-theme music is among the most romantically gorgeous music ever used in a movie. Sometimes his film and serious music overlapped—the final movement of his violin concerto—commissioned and premiered by Jascha Heifetz and dedicated to Alma Mahler Werfel—uses some of the same music heard in 1936's *Anthony Adverse* and *Another Dawn*, 1937's *The Prince and the Pauper*, and 1939's *Juarez*. But since melodies were always swirling around in his head, maybe it was the other way around. Mozart, the composer to whom Korngold was compared in his early years, would walk around with unused themes in his head for years.

In 1947, after scoring seventeen films in fourteen years, Korngold returned to Vienna, having long dreamed of resurrecting his career in his native land. But instead of being welcomed as a hero—or even as grown-up genius—he found that he had become an anachronism. His neo-romantic style was then considered old-fashioned and was received with disinterest or savage criticism, especially the opera *Die Kathrin*, which was finally premiered in Vienna in 1950. He eventually returned to Hollywood; there, too, he had become old-fashioned in less than a decade. Film itself had moved on into a new realism that needed an equally different style of music. So Korngold returned to his classical roots with his Symphony in F-sharp, a cello concerto, several string quartets, and the previously mentioned violin concerto. He even planned a sixth opera.

But by 1957 his health began failing. On November 29, at the age of sixty, he died of a cerebral hemorrhage. Following his death, the Vienna Opera House—the site of his first triumph nearly fifty years earlier—flew a black flag of mourning. When she was told of the gesture, Josephine, his widow, commented, "It's a little late."

Since his death, Korngold's music has been rediscovered and extensively recorded, and with the return of romanticism and adventure to movies, his film music style has been mined by many new Hollywood composers.

Yet at the height of his fame—just before he returned to Vienna and disillusionment in 1947—Korngold had a sense of humor about his success. Sometime before that disappointing return, he encountered fellow Viennese composer Max Steiner at Warner Bros. "Tell me something, Korngold," asked Steiner, who composed, conducted, and orchestrated over three hundred film scores between 1928 and 1965 (among them *The Wizard of Oz*), winning three Oscars. "We've both been at Warner's for ten years now, and in that time your music has gotten progressively worse and worse, and mine has been getting better and better. Why do you suppose that is?" Without missing a beat, Korngold replied in the thickly accented English he never lost, "I'll tell you vy dat iss, Steiner. Dat iss because you are stealing from me and I am stealing from you."

Before buying their home in L.A.'s Pacific Palisades suburb, Charles Laughton and Elsa Lanchester often stayed at Hollywood's most famous (and occasionally infamous) hostelry, the Garden of Allah, as they were in 1933 when this picture was taken.

# 14

## Hollywood's Legendary Odd Couple

### *Charles Laughton and Elsa Lanchester*

How could one not love a Hollywood superstar who once described himself as "having a face like an elephant's behind"? So it's more than a bit ironic that a nude image of the great Charles Laughton, who died in 1962, is listed along with male hotties like Ben Affleck and Brad Pitt as available from at least one Web site.

Luckily, Laughton, unlike Pitt, Affleck, and thousands of actors today and in the past, lacked a press agent. He was conflicted enough within himself without having to deal with the false sense of worth that a press agent frequently creates in a client's mind. Cecil B. DeMille, a man who certainly knew Hollywood as well as anyone, was speaking from personal knowledge when, playing himself in *Sunset Boulevard,* he said, "You know, a dozen press agents working overtime can do terrible things to the human spirit."

Married to the actress Elsa Lanchester from 1929 until his death, Charles Laughton was tortured by his homosexuality, a reality that his wife managed to accept if not condone. He admitted the truth to Lanchester a year after they married, when a male prostitute approached her for more money, but he never publically discussed being gay. That was an unwritten rule in Hollywood at the time, because the studios feared box office damage if a star's homosexuality became public knowledge. And that's why many stars (like Rock Hudson) were forced into sham marriages.

According to some film scholars, Laughton's internalization of his shame of being gay contributed to his mastery as an actor, but in many ways also poisoned his life. If caught in such a net, one would also have to add the fear of losing a career if it were known. For her part, Lanchester never discussed it until she published her autobiography *Elsa Lanchester, Herself* in 1983—fifty-three years after their marriage and more than two decades after Laughton's death.

What is known about Laughton's personal life is somewhat sketchy. In 1950, the year that both Lanchester and Laughton became American citizens, Laughton's nine-year love relationship with David Roberts broke up, and Roberts moved from California to New York. (The pair would always remain devoted friends, and Roberts was one of Laughton's pallbearers.) The actor later met and developed a relationship with Bruce Ashe, a young, successful photographer's model who, like his predecessors, often accompanied the actor to film sets, where Laughton's gayness was more or less accepted. But not by all. Henry Fonda, co-starring in the 1954 Broadway play based on Herman Wouk's Pulitzer Prize-winning novel *The Caine Mutiny*, was apparently so angered by Charles Laughton's direction that he snapped, "What do you know about men, you fat faggot?"

Like his younger brothers Robert (born in 1903) and Francis (born in 1907), Charles Laughton first saw the light of day at the Victoria Hotel in the North Yorkshire town of Scarborough, which was run by his parents Robert and Eliza Laughton. In 1908 the Laughtons bought and moved across the street to the grander Pavilion Hotel.

From his early childhood, Charles knew he would be an actor. He made his debut at fourteen at the Jesuit-run Stonyhurst College, appropriately playing a plump innkeeper in the school's production of the farce *The Private Secretary* (he already had a weight problem). The following year, however, his mother insisted he leave school and train at London's famed Claridge's Hotel, so as to be prepared to take over the family business, started by his paternal grandfather.

In 1917 he—like so many of his compatriots—was called up in World War I, which left him physically and emotionally scarred. He went back to Scarborough and worked for five years in the family hotel with his parents until his father died in 1924, after which he returned to London and entered the Royal Academy of Dramatic Art.

Within two years he evolved into an actor, acknowledged in 1926 with the Bancroft Gold Medal (awarded by the Academy to the finest actor the academy produces in a one-year period), and became a professional. During the year after his debut in Gogol's *The Government Inspector*, he was cast in seven West End productions, among them *Mr. Prohack*, a play based on Arnold Bennett's 1922 novel. It would change his life forever, as well as the life of an actress also cast in the play: Elsa Lanchester. Two years later, on February 10, they were married at London's Registry Office.

In September of 1931 Charles and Elsa made their first voyage to New York, where Charles had been hired to play the role of William Marble, and Elsa his wife Winnie, in Jeffrey Dell's play *Payment Deferred*. (The following year Laughton would star in the movie version of the play, with Ray Milland in one of his early film roles and Maureen O'Sullivan in Lanchester's part.) His Hollywood career then took off like a comet, as did his English career. Even after settling permanently in Hollywood in 1939, the couple virtually commuted back and forth across the Atlantic for years when wartime restrictions permitted it. Nevertheless, they were intimately connected with Hollywood's other émigrés and refugees, particularly the German playwright and poet Bertolt Brecht and the then famous German historical novelist Lion Feuchtwanger and his wife Marta. In fact, Laughton's influence in Hollywood would open many employment doors for the newly arrived refugees.

The year 1932 brought the film that gained Laughton international recognition, Alexander Korda's *The Private Life of Henry VIII* (a reprise of his highly successful starring role in the play, it won him his sole Oscar in 1933). Starting with James Whale's *The Old Dark House,* also made in 1932, Laughton's greatest film work would be in Hollywood.

The intensity he brought to his classic roles is remarkable. High among them was the role of the father in 1934's *The Barretts of Wimpole Street* (when Laughton discovered the studio had toned down the original play's subplot involving his character's incestuous interest in his daughter, played by Maureen O'Sullivan in the movie, Laughton quipped that they "couldn't censor the gleam in his eye") and the role of Captain Bligh in *Mutiny on the Bounty* (certainly the most evil of his portrayals. Co-star Clark Gable's alleged homophobia, which would cause the gay director George Cukor to be fired from *Gone With the Wind* four years later, apparently created so much tension on the set that producer Irving Thalberg had to intervene to restore order).

Laughton's portrayal of the deformed bell-ringer in 1939's *The Hunchback of Notre Dame* is also a classic. A wonderful anecdote relates his method of relaxing during the film. After long—and clearly frustrating—days shooting the movie in unair-conditioned soundstages, Laughton would return to the Garden of Allah Hotel, where he and Lanchester were living at the time, and head directly for the pool. There he would happily splash around for hours with the familiar blissful smile on his face and Quasimodo's hump still strapped to his back, acting as an improvised float.

Laughton's colossal talent is especially evident in a film he made fifteen years later—1955's noir masterpiece *The Night of the Hunter*, a great film and the only one Laughton ever directed. There is a story that Laughton hated children and the film's star, Robert Mitchum, stepped in and directed the scenes with the young Billy Chaplin. Maybe, maybe not. But, according to Mitchum in his autobiography, Laughton so hated the script by the Pulitzer–Prize-winning author James Agee (*A Death in the Family*; he also scripted 1951's *The African Queen* for John Huston) that he rewrote it himself. Because of the film's poor reception, Laughton said he would never direct again; nevertheless, it didn't take long for *Night of the Hunter* to be recognized as one of the true masterpieces of the noir genre.

Even in a film that was never finished, Josef von Sternberg's *I Claudius* (started in 1936 during one of those trans-Atlantic commutes, the project was described in a television special a few years back as "the epic that never was"), Laughton is memorable. As with most of his films, even in this fragment of a movie Laughton's personality reaches right across the screen and grabs the viewer, although it does take a bit of a sense of humor to accept his shameless overacting when he played Nero in one of his early Hollywood films, DeMille's 1932 epic *The Sign of the Cross*.

Even the farce of a marriage was turned into theatrical gold with the loving flippancy Laughton and Lanchester brought to the few films in which they acted together: the comedy shorts *Blue Bottle* and *Day Dreams* (Laughton and Lanchester's first films, made in 1928), Alexander Korda's *Rembrandt* (1936), and 1938's *Vessels of Wrath*.

In 1941 the couple moved into a huge Mediterranean-style home in the Pacific Palisades suburb of Los Angeles that was close to the home of the German refugee historic novelist Lion Feuchtwanger and his wife, Marta, who frequently hosted the Laughtons in their sprawling home. He was also close to the Santa Monica Canyon home of the gay émigré British novelist Christopher Isherwood, with whom he could feel comfortable about his sexuality.

Los Angeles, like many cities, seems to love destroying its cultural monuments, and this house of the Laughtons was nearly lost—first by neglect and second to the destructive 1993 earthquake and the subsequent vandalism that reduced it to a shell of its former self. Bought (by a person who didn't know who the previous owners were) and recently restored, today it stands as a vivid reminder of the forceful personalities of both of these actors.

In its time the house was the site of Laughton's private acting classes, attended by Robert Ryan, Shelley Winters, and her roommate Marilyn Monroe. (Laughton would later cast Winters in *Night of the Hunter*.)

It was also where, over a two-year period, Laughton (who spoke no German) and Bertolt Brecht (who spoke little English) somehow fashioned an English translation of Brecht's earlier play *Galileo*; in July of 1947, six months before it opened in New York, Laughton starred in a legendary staging of the work at the Coronet Theater on La Cienega Boulevard near Beverly Hills.

Despite their language difficulties, Brecht and Laughton—both possessing somewhat cantankerous personalities—got along famously. Laughton was a dedicated gardener, and Brecht celebrated this passion (along with the house) in a humorous poem called "Garden in Progress."

> High above the Pacific coast below it
> The waves' gentle thunder and the rumble of oil tankers
> Lies the actor's garden.
> Nor did the lord of the garden take in only
> His own plants and trees but also
> The plants and trees of his neighbors;
> When told this
> Smiling he admitted: I steal from all sides.

Laughton's flowers, plants, and trees are long gone, of course, but the home's new owner has replaced them with many tropical plants, giving the place a lush ambiance today.

Like many actors, the Laughtons liked to entertain. In her autobiography, Shelley Winters celebrates this aspect of the couple's lifestyle, recalling memorable evenings in the company of such golden age stars as Charlie Chaplin, with his soon-to-be-ex-wife Paulette Goddard, and Peter Ustinov.

Few today remember that Laughton was an important art collector. "All over the walls of the living room and dining room were gorgeous paintings of fat naked ladies," Winters added in her autobiography of Laughton's collection of paintings by the French impressionist Pierre-Auguste Renoir; the artist's son, film director Jean Renoir

(*Grand Illusion*), was a friend of the actor and aided him in collecting many of his father's works. Laughton also collected modern art and was an early fan of pre-Columbian artifacts. Broadcaster Norman Corwin once wrote a poem about his collection:

> This is a house of art
> In every part
> In the master's can
> Cezanne;
> On the kitchen wall
> Maillol;
> Wherever you park your ass, O
> It's under a Picasso.

In midlife Laughton began making appearances as a reader and storyteller, begun with live readings for wounded soldiers recuperating at the Birmingham Hospital in Los Angeles's San Fernando Valley during World War II. These "one-man guided tours" (as he called them) were hugely successful for several reasons: Laughton loved introducing writers he admired to audiences, and audiences, as well as Laughton, enjoyed the intimate settings. Such readings were on occasion turned into staged evenings like his Broadway appearance in 1951 reading Shaw's *Don Juan in Hell.* This activity reached its apex when, for the huge viewing audience of *The Ed Sullivan Show* in the 1950s, he garnered large ratings by reading from the Bible.

But not every professional decision was so successful for Laughton. In 1959 he decided to realize a longtime dream by appearing as *King Lear* at Stratford-upon-Avon. Despite the starry cast (his Cordelia was Zoe Caldwell, and the Fool was played by the young Ian Holm), the reviews were devastating; Laughton's credibility in the role seems to have been largely undermined by his weight.

In 1961 he attempted a reading tour with his lover Bruce Ashe, but had to be hospitalized after a fall in the bath. During his hospital stay, his doctors discovered he had spinal cancer. After fighting the disease for a year, Charles Laughton died on December 15, 1962, at the Hollywood home that he and Elsa had moved to after selling their Pacific Palisades house in 1949.

She was a bohemian, a rebel, and, in effect, Charles Laughton's beard. She was friends with H. G. Wells and Evelyn Waugh. Onstage she played witches, a larva, Anne of Cleves, Ariel in *The Tempest*, and Peter Pan. Her film career included roles in *Mary Poppins, Witness for the Prosecution, Bell, Book, and Candle*, and *Lassie Come Home.*

But Elsa Lanchester is best remembered for one of her shortest film appearances—a tour de force acting turn as Monster's wife (complete with Brillo-frizzed hair) in 1935's *The Bride of Frankenstein . . .* her shriek when the Monster touches her is, along with that of Faye Ray in the original *King Kong*, certainly one of the most famous movie screams ever. (In the prelude of *The Bride of Frankenstein*, Lanchester also does a rather subdued turn—for her, anyway—as *Frankenstein*'s author, Mary Shelley.) The movie was directed by James Whale, who three years earlier directed Laughton in his first Hollywood movie. (Whale's life would be chronicled—Hollywood style—in the 1998 film *Gods and Monsters*, starring Ian McKellen as the gay director.)

Elsa Lanchester was born on October 28, 1902, in London, the second child of James Sullivan, a factory worker and later commercial clerk, and Edith Lanchester. Her parents were militant socialists, pacifists, and vegetarians, who caused a scandal when, true to their free love beliefs, they decided to live together in 1895 without marrying. Edith's family was so outraged that they kidnapped her in collusion with a psychiatrist, who committed her to a lunatic asylum. Her cause was soon taken up by fellow members of the Social Democratic Federation, England's first Marxist organization (she had been secretary to Karl Marx's daughter, Eleanor), and her release was secured when she was found not to be insane.

Unsurprisingly, Elsa Lanchester was brought up in a family environment that stressed rebellion and nonconformity. She received little formal schooling, but her precocious talent for dancing led to a scholarship at the age of eleven to Isadora Duncan's Bellevue School in Paris, where her attendance was ended by the First World War. Lanchester then began to teach dancing, and after the war opened the Children's Theater, recruiting local children for musical entertainments. In 1921 it was shut down, allegedly for violating child labor laws. Then she co-founded a nightclub, devoted to presenting late-night cabaret and avant-garde plays, that became a fashionable haunt for bohemian London (of which she was surely a part), paying her way by working as an artist's model for, among others, England's great sculptor Jacob Epstein and, it is claimed, occasionally posing as a corespondent in divorce cases.

Her first theatrical appearance was in a one-acter, *Thirty Minutes in a Street*, in 1922, followed by playing a larva in the Capek brothers' *The Insect Play*. She first appeared on celluloid in an amateur film made in 1924 by her friend Evelyn Waugh. In 1927, the same year she met her future husband in the play *Mr. Prohack*, she made three short films that another friend, H. G. Wells, had written for her.

The few appearances with her husband—both in plays and films— were memorable. The first in America was on Broadway in 1932 in *Payment Deferred*. She appeared as Anne of Cleves in *The Private Life of Henry VIII,* after which the couple remained in England, acting together in the 1933 Old Vic season, where she was highly praised as Ariel in Shakespeare's *The Tempest* (Laughton played Prospero). In 1936, as earlier mentioned, she appeared opposite her husband in *Rembrandt*, as well as on the London stage as Peter Pan (with Laughton as Captain Hook). Her Peter Pan, incidently, was the last to be approved by the author, J. M. Barrie.

Because of her somewhat eccentric appearance, her film career tended toward playing eccentric and character parts. In 1949 Lanchester was nominated for the Best Supporting Actress Oscar for her appearance in the Loretta Young/Celeste Holm vehicle *Come to the Stable* (Lanchester played an artist) and again in 1958 for her performance playing her husband's nurse in *Witness for the Prosecution.*

Despite her film activities, Lanchester's heart was always set on the stage. In fact, claiming that she (unlike her husband) lacked the ambition for great film roles, she once told a British interviewer, "I only wanted to do vaudeville. . . . I like to get a laugh. I'm a vaudevillian, not an actor." For a decade beginning in 1941, she appeared in cabaret at Los Angeles's Turnabout Theater, later touring her act to packed houses across the country. In 1960 Laughton directed her in a successful one-woman show, *Elsa Lanchester, Herself,* which had a short run on Broadway (the show's name also served as the title of her 1983 autobiography). After Laughton's death, she continued to act in films and television (including episodes of such hit shows as *Moonlighting* and *Mannix*), as well as maintaining her cabaret appearances.

Elsa Lanchester died of pneumonia in Los Angeles the day after Christmas in 1986.

In the 1920s émigré architect Rudolf Schindler wrote his Vienna classmate and friend Richard Neutra, "Come to Los Angeles. . . . They're building a new city here." Neutra followed his advice. Although the pair didn't remain friends, they did, along with such homegrown talent as Frank Lloyd Wright, change American architecture, making it, to use Neutra's term, "mentally footloose." The result, iconically exemplified by his first commission, Hollywood's famous Lovell House, remains a showcase for Neutra's philosophy that homes should be open to the outdoors—physically, visually, and emotionally.

# 15
·······

# The Architects

## *Richard Neutra and Rudolf Schindler*

To paraphrase the late comedian Rodney Dangerfield, architects get no respect. In the long run, anyway, it seems. How many residents of Los Angeles realize that the otherwise functional Emerson Junior High School in West Los Angeles was designed by one of the giants of modern architecture, Richard Neutra? Do residents of Hollywood know that the popular Beachwood Market was designed (in 1954) by another famous architecht, John Lautner? Worse, considering the civic and private ennui that has met the desperately needed plea for money to save the crumbling Ennis-Brown house in Hollywood, one of Frank Lloyd Wright's greatest creations (thus, by definition, one of the greatest house designs in the world), does anyone really care?

They should. Outside of personal relationships and jobs, few things affect the quality of life more than our built environment. Is anything more depressing than a walk on the environmental wild side through crumbling neighborhoods in one of our major cities. Or is there anything more stimulating to the quality of life than a visit to architect Frank Gehry's glorious Disney Concert Hall in Los Angeles or its similarly free-form predecessor in Bilbao, Spain?

Since the beginning of civilization—perhaps even before—humankind has been building for all kinds of reasons: to impress (both for governmental, as well as religious purposes), to shelter, to protect (castles and fortresses), and even to enable communications (the Roman road system). But what they didn't do was deliberately build something that would seemingly contradict the very reason a building or a house was built in the first place: to include the outdoors as part of the indoor environment—physically, visually, and emotionally. That happened in Los Angeles, and that it happened at all was due in large part to the efforts of two immigrants.

In the early 1920s, the Vienna-born architect Rudolf Schindler, then supervising the construction of Aline Barnsdall's now celebrated Hollyhock House for his mentor Frank Lloyd Wright, wrote his friend Richard Neutra (also born and educated in Vienna, where they had met in architecture school), "Come to Los Angeles. They're building a new city here."

And, eventually, Neutra and his wife, Dione, arrived via Chicago, where they spent time with Frank Lloyd Wright. "After I had been in New York, Chicago, and Taliesin (Wright's home in Spring Green, Wisconsin) more or less as Mr. Wright's guest," Neutra wrote in his rather pompous 1962 autobiography *Life and Shape*, "I began to think about California, as he had no work or projects going. I made up my mind in the winter of 1925."

Why California? Well, for one thing, there was the invitation from Schindler, who, with his wife, had come to Los Angeles in 1920, and in 1921 and '22 had built one of the iconic homes of the century for himself and his wife on Kings Road in what is now West Hollywood. Neutra had also been attracted earlier by a poster in a travel office on the Bahnhofstrasse in Zurich featuring a palm tree and the message "California Calls You."

"On the way," he recalled, "my family—I and my wife Dione, two of our children, and my mother-in-law—marveled at the Grand Canyon" while their three-month-old son, in their hotel room with a nurse, tore up their travel guide for the western United States. "So we arrived at the coast unadvised and unprepared," he added. But not friendless; they soon moved in with the Schindlers.

Although the couples did not remain friends (living together in the fairly small house took care of that, and there are many stories of wife swapping that cannot be entirely confirmed), the two architects would spend the rest of their lives creating homes and buildings that, like Frank Lloyd Wright's work, gave an entirely new direction to architecture in America.

In the beginning all was sweetness and light, the couple buoyed by the excitement that attends any major move. Neutra had developed a theory of naturalistic architecture and felt that in the subtropical Southern California climate and cultural environment it could be developed. "In California," he said, "I found what I had hoped for. A people who were more 'mentally footloose' than those elsewhere, people who did not mind deviating opinions as long as they were not political. All this [seemed] to provide a good climate for trying something independent of hidebound habituation—European or even American—and for getting acquainted with human minds and patterns of behavior in a sort of tropical exfoliation."

The "new city" that Schindler said was being built in Los Angeles was a product of a building boom that would last until World War II and has rarely been equaled since. It included not only modern structures, but also thousands of Mediterranean and Spanish-style villas, as well as back-to-basics Arts and Crafts designs.

In many ways Hollywood's spirit for building during the early part of the twentieth century, as in Manhattan in the last third of the nineteenth century, was not unlike that of Renaissance Florence. Driven by economic success, the heady rediscovery of ancient culture, and civic pride, Florentines—or at least those in the forefront of the boom like the Medici—were also building a new city. In the process, they erected some of the most palatial and architecturally important residences and public buildings ever constructed by one people in one place at one time. Much of what they built (as well as what the newly rich built in the Eastern United States in the late nineteenth century) still stands as a monument to boundless optimism and the money available to demonstrate it. But there was a major difference between what Florence and New York built and what happened in Hollywood.

Unlike the Florentine example, Hollywood's boom was driven not by a rediscovered cultural heritage, but by something entirely new. Its coin was not a solid verity like lire or ducats or dollars, but the antithesis of the seriousness hitherto implied by architecture. Much of it was driven by fantasy.

So it's not surprising that much of what was built in Hollywood was not sheer looniness, but an often intellectual, indeed frequently joyful, celebration of newfound freedom from traditional architecture and design. Schindler, less facile at coining a phrase like Neutra's "mentally footloose," simply saw Los Angeles as an earthly paradise with the perfect environment (including money, outlook, and as he and other avant-garde architects would memorably exploit, climate) to develop the next stage of modern architecture.

And the influence of this new architecture spread fast. It took a century or so for the Renaissance to move from Florence to Northern Europe. It took less than a decade for Hollywood's "mentally footloose" architectural and design innovations to conquer the world. Why? Hollywood's very reason for being—the movies. Would the Art Deco movement's worldwide popularity in the 1930s have been as powerful without being endlessly portrayed in the glamorously escapist film sets of the era?

True, some industry leaders like Cecil B. DeMille (who arrived in Hollywood in 1913) opted for the eclectically traditional in the palatial home he built in the new Laughlin Park enclave. (Its style has been laughingly described by the present owners as "Midwest Mediterranean.") So did Columbia's Harry Cohn and actors like Tyrone Power, Errol Flynn, and many others; traditional architecture was a reminder of the world in which they were raised.

But as the success of Hollywood's newly rich was rooted in fantasy, much of what many others built was also founded on escapism and experimentation: houses built to resemble Mayan temples, an entire development deliberately designed to resemble an Italian hill town (Whitley Heights), Japanese teahouses, French châteaus, Italian palazzos, and romantic Spanish villas with courtyards complete with splashing fountains. (Hence, too, hot dog stands built to resemble hot dogs, and a Coca-Cola bottling plant built like an ocean liner because ships then possessed sanitary connotations.) And many of the houses and buildings were, for the first time in design history, visually open to the outdoors, an element that also played a major part in their design. A perfect example is the seemingly all-glass Wayfarer's Chapel on the Palos Verdes Peninsula, designed by Frank Lloyd Wright, Jr., in 1951.

Neutra's first commission, a private home, was one of the most evocative of his new theories of design and his philosophy that architecture should be a force for social betterment. It remains one of the finest houses of the new style in the United States and, when it was built, created such a sensation in architectural circles that it became the first house to spread what would be a transforming architectural message to Europe.

At the time, 1927, Neutra referred to it as the "Health House," so named because of his "deep interest in biological fitness," which was shared by the client, Dr. Philip M. Lovell, who wrote a regular health and fitness column for the *Los Angeles Times*. Today the house is universally known as the "Lovell House" and is familiar to fans of the 1997 film *L.A. Confidential*, where it was used as the home of Pierce Patchett, a man who supplies call girls whose features have been altered to resemble those of major movie stars.

Still, Neutra had a lot of ground breaking to do. Despite the excitement over Frank Lloyd Wright's cement-block houses built a few years earlier in Los Angeles, it was still a city defined as much by Spanish Revival architecture. But—and here is where luck comes into things—Mrs. Lovell's sister was married to Samuel Freeman, for whom Frank Lloyd Wright had designed a cement-block home in Hollywood (still standing, it is being restored by the University of

Southern California architecture school). Schindler, who supervised the building of Wright's Hollyhock House, started in 1916 and completed four years later, had lived for a time in the one-room apartment below the garage of the Freeman house and even designed some of the built-in furniture before the relationship broke up. And when Schindler couldn't or wouldn't design the Lovell house, the job fell easily to Neutra because of the advanced design philosophy the pair shared.

Neutra, who was convinced that mankind would eventually run out of level ground for buildings, was excited and challenged by the precipitous site Lovell had purchased near Griffith Park. According to the architect, his client could also see the future in Neutra's suspended steel skeleton design. It was a revolutionary design, as well as probably the first in America to provide—in line with Lovell's fitness thinking—a fusion of indoor and outdoor living that also allowed, via large windows, making the outside vistas part of the interior design. It certainly wasn't easy to do—the house's skeleton had to be fabricated in sections and transported by trucks to the steep hillside site.

Working with the Lovells caused Neutra to rethink not only the largely Victorian kitchen arrangements of the era (because of the Lovell's naturopathic diet of largely raw food), but also the home's ventilation and illumination, and to provide a relatively new accessory at that time—a swimming pool. For a housewarming, Dr. Lovell literally invited the entire city, and thousands showed up.

Neutra didn't rest on his laurels, however. In 1935 he designed a sinuously Moderne house for filmmaker Josef von Sternberg (then famous for directing Marlene Dietrich in most of her movies) in Northridge in the San Fernando Valley. Instead of the large number of rooms common at the time, the house had only a few and only one bedroom. Neutra was famous for paying attention to his clients' desires rather than imposing his artistic vision on them (basically the opposite of Frank Lloyd Wright's philosophy), yet even he was amused by von Sternberg's demand that none of the bathroom doors in the house should have locks. Sternberg, well acquainted with the frequently theatrical behavior of many actors, claimed he wanted to prevent his party guests from locking themselves in a bathroom and threatening to commit suicide. Sadly, the house was torn down in 1972 to make way for a housing development.

Neutra had a great sense of humor and would sometimes make fun of his clients by telling outrageous lies about them—always with a straight face—to, as he said, "make things more interesting." In the case of von Sternberg, who had a reputation for being an unbending autocrat, he often repeated the story that the director kept cannons and poisonous spiders at the house to scare off intruders, and that he had asked Neutra to design an incinerator to dispose of the bodies his chauffeur removed every morning from the electrified moat around the house.

In 1946 Neutra designed another of his iconic homes for Edgar Kaufmann, the man for whom Frank Lloyd Wright earlier designed his famous Falling Water house in Pennsylvania. The house, located in Palm Springs, is an even greater exponent of Neutra's innovation of using the outdoor landscape as part of the interior design via huge areas of glass.

Richard Neutra died in Wuppertal, Germany, in 1970. His son, Dion, also an architect and once his father's partner, has carried on his father's architectural tradition in Los Angeles.

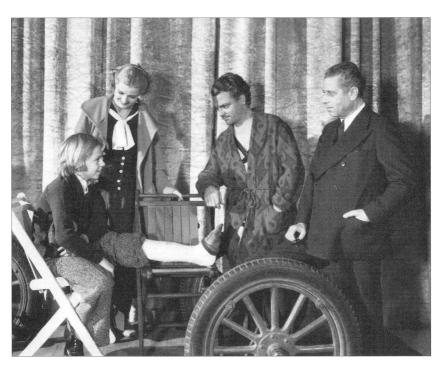

Max Reinhardt (far right) on the set of 1935's film version of his hugely successful Hollywood Bowl production of *A Midsummer Night's Dream.* Cast members include (from left to right) the thirteen-year-old Mickey Rooney (who appeared as Puck), Anita Louise (Titania), and James Cagney (Bottom).

# 16

·······

# The Theater's Genius

## Max Reinhardt

In 1934 the famous Viennese producer and director Max Reinhardt produced what remains one of the most celebrated events in the Hollywood Bowl's history—a ten-day run of Shakespeare's *A Midsummer Night's Dream* that drew over two hundred thousand spectators. In an innovative move, he cast several Hollywood stars for the production, as opposed to theatrical actors, among them the thirteen-year-old Mickey Rooney as Puck. This produced the intended result of attracting film fans to the performances, as well as providing another, unplanned benefit.

For many of Hollywood's otherwise elitist émigrés, the phenomenal success of the project placed the imprimatur of theatrical respectability on Hollywood's film industry. In effect, Reinhardt proved that even in Hollywood—then and to an extent still thought of by many intellectuals as hopelessly provincial—people of all cultural backgrounds and educational attainments will turn out for a good show.

It wasn't just a good show, though; it was a great show. Reinhardt's secret, as he had proved over and over again in Europe, was to combine the sumptuous staging that he had trademarked in European theaters and at the Salzburg Music Festival (which he co-founded in 1922) with great direction.

As Mickey Rooney recalled in his 1965 autobiography, "I was introduced to [the role of] Puck . . . by a man who spoke no English. His name was Max Reinhardt. He was a great German [sic] director who happened to be Jewish so that, at the suggestion of the management, he left his native country [and] came to California to produce and direct *A Midsummer Night's Dream* at the Hollywood Bowl.

"The community of Hollywood was vastly excited at the first hint that he might be coming," Rooney continued, "for Max Reinhardt had done superb things in the European theater—things that were at once imaginative and daring. And if there were two things Hollywood wasn't in 1934, those were it. Imaginative and daring. In making motion pictures I mean. Naturally people admire someone with more courage than they [have]. Reinhardt was a hero before he got off the train."

Rooney continued, "When Reinhardt announced that he would audition for *A Midsummer Night's Dream*, actors raced down from the hills. Olivia de Havilland wanted to be Puck. Although Puck is male, Olivia was only eighteen years old, and in proper costuming could have passed for a boy. Mary Pickford wanted to play Puck. She was forty years old (actually she was forty-two according to most biographers), but still slim. I was signed to play Puck. Me. Mickey Rooney. Aged thirteen."

Actually, de Havilland had been spotted playing Puck in a Northern California community theater production of Shakespeare's play. Although she planned a career as an English teacher, Reinhardt convinced her to become the understudy for Gloria Stuart, originally cast as Hermia. When Stuart dropped out, de Havilland, who would become celebrated five years later when Warner Bros., with whom she had signed a contract after the play, loaned her to MGM, where she played the angelic Melanie Wilkes in David O. Selznick's *Gone With the Wind*, earning an Oscar nomination for Best Supporting Actress. Many Hollywood careers came about in similarly unexpected ways, of course.

"Although I had been onstage for more than eleven years, Reinhardt's was the first outstanding direction ever given me," Rooney concluded. "Honestly I don't believe I have ever worked for a comparably outstanding director. Not one. If I had, I would be a better actor today."

Co-opting members of the film industry for the cast was nothing compared to what Reinhardt did with the play; among the innovations, he had the bowl shell moved out of sight and transformed the stage into a forest glade. In his 1979 biography of his father, Gottfried Reinhardt recalls, "That Max Reinhardt knew how to put on *A Midsummer Night's Dream* surprised nobody. The most astonishing feat was the technical *coup de main.* I remember how, intrigued by the natural coulisse, he worked out a torch parade for the last act, stepping to Mendelssohn's 'Wedding March' from the heights of the Hollywood Hills to the bottom of the valley across a specially built bridge onto a scene that seemed suspended in free nature.

"It did not concern him," Gottfried continued, "in Southern California's tinder-dry vegetation that this constituted a fire hazard of the first order. How difficult people found it to deny him a wish is proved by the OK from the Los Angeles Fire Department.

"At the dress rehearsal, the torchbearers reached their destination two hours after the play had ended," Gottfried added. "They could not find their way through the pathless brush in the dark. All the participants begged my father to renounce such manifest lunacy. But lunacy and miracle seem not so far apart; at the opening, the torchbearers arrived on the terrace of Theseus's palace on the dot, and with the final bar of the march, assumed their prescribed stance."

None of this would have happened, of course, had Reinhardt not found the money to mount the show. And he did it with the kind of muscle producers have found effective for generations—get the town's five-hundred-pound gorilla on your side. In Los Angeles, that meant Harry Chandler, the publisher of the all-powerful *Los Angeles Times.* And what Chandler did was to put the arm on the city's film studios. "Contrary to the gloomy prophecies of the film moguls who had unenthusiastically yielded to Harry Chandler . . . to underwrite the $125,000 guarantee for the venture, and had warned the public would stay away from it," Gottfried Reinhardt adds, "the undertaking was an unprecedented hit."

The problem with theatrical productions is that after they close, they can only be revisited in memory, reminiscences of audience members, or old production shots. That is, unless, like Leonard Bernstein's *West Side Story,* they are made into film, but that wasn't a common practice in the mid-1930s by any means. But, happily, that is exactly what happened with Reinhardt's *A Midsummer Night's Dream*, which was made into an enchanting film by Warner Bros. in 1935. Co-directed by Reinhardt and William Dieterle (*Dr. Ehrlich's Magic Bullet, 1940*; *Elephant Walk, 1954*), it has been described as "black and white magic; the zenith of fantasy." And, in many ways, it is.

Some members of the stage cast repeated their roles, but several new Hollywood actors were added, including comedian Joe E. Brown as Flute, Victor Jory as Oberon, James Cagney as Bottom, and Dick Powell as Lysander. Luckily, de Havilland remained as Hermia, and Mickey Rooney as Puck, his performance demonstrating how enchanting he must have been in the Bowl performances. Reinhardt also invited the Viennese composer Erich Korngold to come to Hollywood to adapt Felix Mendelssohn's incidental music for the play, composed in 1843, to the 114-minute length of the movie. This would prove a career-making event in Korngold's life; returning to Hollywood in 1937, he would become one of the most successful composers of movie scores of the era.

The film won two Oscars: Cinematography for Hal Mohr, the only write-in candidate ever to win an Oscar, and Film Editing. It was, however, banned in Germany because of Reinhardt's and Mendelssohn's Jewish ancestry.

In 1920 Max Reinhardt stunned Berliners with a production of the nineteenth-century warhorse of the French Revolution *Danton's Tod* (*Danton's Death*), staged only a year after the 1919 German Revolution that established the Weimar Republic. Kurt Tucholsky, a poet of the time, described the impact of the production in verse, reading in part:

Act Three was great in Reinhardt's play, Six hundred extras milling.
Listen to what the critics say! All Berlin finds it thrilling.
The stage is shaking. The audience rocks. The whole thing is over by nine o'clock.

Soon, with the composer Richard Strauss and the German poet and (Strauss) librettist Hugo von Hofmannsthal, Reinhardt would create one of his longest-lasting legacies: the Salzburg Festival. Other than for a few wartime interruptions, it remains one of the most acclaimed classical music celebrations. The first event of the festival, which opened in 1922, was Reinhardt's staging of the medieval English morality play *Everyman* in the city's seventeenth-century cathedral square; the play remains part of the festival's schedule. The next season saw the first performances of operas by the town's favorite son, Wolfgang Amadeus Mozart, whose music is still the backbone of the festival. Since its beginnings, many world-famous conductors have been closely identified with Salzburg, including Arturo Toscanini and Bruno Walter in the 1930s and, more recently, the late Herbert von Karajan, who added an Easter season.

Max Reinhardt was born Maximilian Goldmann in Baden bei Wien, Austria (a suburb of Vienna, as the name implies), on September 9, 1873. He was the eldest of seven children born to an Orthodox Jewish couple, Wilhelm and Rose Goldmann, who wanted him to become a banker. Nevertheless, they were wise enough to allow him to follow his fascination with the theater after being urged to do so by a member of the Vienna Burgtheater. He began his career at the age of seventeen as actor and assistant director at the Salzburg State Theater. In 1894 he moved to the Deutsches Theater in Berlin, which from 1905 he directed. Also that year he became famous overnight within the German theatrical community with his first staging of *A Midsummer Night's Dream*.

The following year Reinhardt built the Kammerspiele next door, where chamber dramas were produced in a minimalist and naturalistic style. Before leaving Germany shortly after the Nazis came to power, he had staged over six hundred productions of plays and operettas, including twenty-two Shakespearean plays. It was, in fact, Reinhardt's Berlin production of Oscar Wilde's *Salome* that convinced Richard Strauss that he was on the right track turning it into an opera in 1903. In 1922 Bertolt Brecht, with whom Reinhardt would reunite in Los Angeles, was brought on as a creative consultant to the Deutsches Theater. Reinhardt also toured the troupe, taking it to New York in 1914 and 1927–28.

It is hardly remembered anymore, but it was Reinhardt who gave the late photographer Leni Riefenstahl her first professional job when he hired her as a dancer (her planned career) to appear at the Deutsches Theater. That career ended abruptly when she injured her knee and turned to film acting before turning to photography and filmmaking herself. It was, in fact, her notorious 1934 documentary *Triumph of the Will* and the subsequent documentary of the 1936 Berlin Olympics, that nearly destroyed her career. Both films won gold medals in subsequent film competitions in Paris and Vienna. She died in 2003 only weeks after celebrating her hundred-and-first birthday with Las Vegas performers Siegfried and Roy.

Far more significant, however, was the influence Reinhardt had on the film styles of F. W. Murnau (*Nosferatu*, considered one of the greatest horror films, made in 1922), the celebrated Ernst Lubitsch, and Otto Preminger, all of whom enjoyed major careers in Hollywood.

Because of Reinhardt's disappointment over the reception of the film version of *A Midsummer Night's Dream*, he devoted the rest of his days to the theater. After settling in the Hollywood after first fleeing Germany for Austria, and then fleeing that country before the Anschluss in March 1938, Reinhardt opened an acting school for "stage, screen and radio" hopefuls. Among his many students who went on to enjoy major careers were Robert Ryan (who also studied with Charles Laughton, a neighbor in the Pacific Palisades) and Nanette Fabray. Far more famous, however, was a student who had to audition several times before he allowed her to enroll in his Berlin acting school. As it turned out, she would have the most illustrious career of any of his students, starring in many films before settling in Hollywood and becoming a cabaret entertainer. Her name? Marlene Dietrich.

But Reinhardt was not happy in Los Angeles. His former wife, the actress Helene Thimig, to whom he was married from 1917 until 1933 and who assisted him in the administration of the theater workshop, once wrote about his disappointment after the school closed in 1941, ". . . our stagings (inevitably less sumptuous than those in Berlin and Salzburg—and the Hollywood Bowl, of course) were almost entirely unnoticed. With prominent people of the film industry, this kind of neglect was painful, but it didn't surprise us. With the émigrés, however, this kind of attitude seemed more disappointing."

Reinhardt then opened a theater workshop in New York, but it was also a disappointment . . . time, style, and his own fame had passed him by. Max Reinhardt died in New York on October 31, 1943.

Today Los Angeles possesses a lively theater environment that is the envy of many cities. In fact, when Max Reinhardt was struggling to improve the theater life in the city, it already had a pretty good one—it just wasn't what he had been used to in Berlin or Salzburg. Perhaps he would have had a more successful career if he had pursued film direction or lived long enough to enjoy the postwar boom in all fields—including cultural.

Nevertheless, one cannot help but notice the irony in Reinhardt's fate: in a place where thousands of his fellow refugees found happiness, success, and fulfillment while doing exactly what Reinhardt wanted to do—changing the very fabric of the city's (and, to an extent, the country's) cultural life—Reinhardt, for all his talent, failed. His *envoi* was bitter. "In a city where the surface seems to dominate everything else—the surface of the film screen," he wrote toward the end of his life, "you justifiably can't expect an interest in the three-dimensional art of the theater."

After Reinhardt's death, his former wife, Helene Thimig, appeared in several films, including 1944's *None But the Lonely Heart* with Cary Grant and the following year's *Isle of the Dead* with Boris Karloff. She died in 1974.

Today Reinhardt's memory is carried on most vitally by Vienna's Max Reinhardt Seminar, generally considered the best German-language theater school.

Arnold Schoenberg, today recognized as a musical prophet, perhaps had good reason for his stern pose in this portrait (taken in the late 1930s). Despite his great gifts, Schoenberg had to struggle to support his family. When forced to retire from his professorship at UCLA for health reasons, his pension was $40.38 monthly.

# 17

## The Modernist Musicians

### *Arnold Schoenberg, Eric Zeisl, Ernst Krenek, and Ernst Toch*

Unlike the émigré and refugee writers, most of whom came from Germany, all of the refugee composers of serious music were Austrian. And the most eminent among them was Arnold Schoenberg.

Ask the man or woman on the street today who Arnold Schoenberg was, and you will almost certainly get a blank stare. Such was not the case among classical music fans in the 1940s (when there seems to have been a lot more of them). Some considered Schoenberg one of the most exciting talents around, whose compositions were creating a new musical language, unshackled by centuries of tradition. However, most of the music-going public, who then, as now, preferred pretty tunes to cerebral compositions, rejected his unharmonious melodies as cacophony.

To followers like modernist composers Anton Webern and Alban Berg, Schoenberg was both a hero and a prophet. He was reputed to be a very prickly and difficult man to know and befriend, a man who "never smiled," according to one observer. Because of a much maligned comment about the experimental twelve-tone music composition system he invented years earlier, he was also thought of as hopelessly egotistical. "I have today made a discovery," he said, "which will ensure the supremacy of German music for the next hundred years."

Most believe that, rather than reflecting ego, his remark was a product of a wry and ironic sense of humor, little known to other than close friends. As proof, they offer the fact that Charlie Chaplin, the film industry's greatest exponent of wry and ironic humor, was one of Schoenberg's closest friends. Certainly a 1937 offer by MGM's Irving Thalberg was received by the composer in a manner what could only be classified as wry and ironic.

It seems that Thalberg, then chief of production at the studio (where he was nicknamed "Czar of all the Rushes"), heard a New York Philharmonic broadcast performance of Schoenberg's *Verklärte Nacht* (*Transfigured Night*), a Wagnerian-style piece composed in 1899, some years before Schoenberg developed his atonal system. Thalberg called him into his office, accompanied by Salka Viertel, then an MGM screenwriter, as a translator, and invited him to compose the score for *The Good Earth*, a planned film version of Pearl Buck's best-selling novel about a Chinese peasant who becomes rich but loses his wife in the process.

"Think of it," Thalberg reportedly said to the dubious composer. "There is a terrific storm going on, the wheat field is swaying in the wind, and suddenly the earth begins to tremble. In the midst of the earthquake, O-lan gives birth. Can you imagine such an opportunity for music?"

"With so much going on," Schoenberg quipped, "what do you need music for?"

Reportedly, Thalberg also said that he wanted "oriental music" and added, "Do me one favor, one little favor. Should we get together on this, please don't write music that is too ugly, would you?" By 1937 news of Schoenberg's atonal music had reached Thalberg.

"But, Herr Thalberg," the composer said, hopefully with a smile. "Haven't you heard that I only write ugly music?"

Nevertheless, as Schoenberg was—as usual—strapped for money, he decided to see how far he could push the film mogul. His annual UCLA salary was five thousand dollars, a good amount in that post-depression year, but not enough to comfortably cover the expenses of raising three children in a Brentwood house that formerly belonged to

Shirley Temple. Several days later Schoenberg contacted Thalberg and said he would do it if he had total control of the film's sound, including the dialogue. He explained that he planned to have the actors speak in the same pitch and key as his music and follow strictly assigned cadences. "It would be similar to my *Pierrot Lunaire*," he said, referring to his 1912 song cycle composed in a speaking-singing style. Oh yes, he also asked for fifty thousand dollars for the job. "Fortunately, [it was] too much money," the composer later reminisced, "for it would have been the end of me."

Born in Vienna on September 13, 1874, Arnold Schoenberg began violin lessons when he was eight and almost immediately started composing. From 1901 until 1903, he was in Berlin as a cabaret musician, although he continued composing (his symphonic poem *Pelleas und Melisande* and giant *Gurrelieder* date from those years). After returning to Vienna, caught up in the ferment of the discovery of abstract expressionism, as well as the new behavioral theories of Sigmund Freud, he began taking students (Berg and Webern were among the first) and changing his musical style from the lushly romantic to the spare, complex, and harmonically somewhat alien-sounding style that would be his hallmark until he returned to tonal composition after moving to Los Angeles a generation later.

It was, according to Schoenberg himself, military service during World War I that disrupted his life and changed his music. Following the Armistice, he worked at evolving a means of order that would enable his musical texture to become simpler and clearer, and this resulted in the "method of composition with twelve tones," in which the twelve semitonal intervals are regarded as equal and no one note or tonality is given the emphasis it occupied in classical harmony. "Had times been normal [before and after 1914], then the music of our time would have been very different," he said.

Some of this is personal revisionism; he actually was searching for a new style of music when he composed the short, turbulent opera for soprano *Erwartung* (*Expectation*) in 1909. It was not premiered until 1924. Schoenberg returned to Berlin in 1925, but as a Jewish musician, was obligated to leave the capital in 1933, his gigantic opera *Moses und Aron* unfinished. He moved to Paris and formally returned to the Jewish faith, which he had deserted for Lutheranism in 1898. Later the same year he arrived in the United States and worked at a conservatory in Boston for a time before settling in Los Angeles in 1934.

After first working as a professor of composition at the University of Southern California, Schoenberg was hired by UCLA in 1936 on the recommendation of Otto Klemperer, then music director of the Los Angeles Philharmonic. "Dr. Schoenberg is the most important figure among contemporary musicians," Klemperer wrote. "I am convinced that he is the greatest living music teacher we have in the world." Nevertheless, Schoenberg was rarely able to convince Klemperer to program his music. "At first he was furious because I didn't perform him more," Klemperer commented to writer Peter Heyworth in 1973. "I constantly had to explain that the Los Angeles public was not yet ready for him."

While in Los Angeles, Schoenberg continued working on *Moses und Aron*, but despite his tight finances and the frustration of teaching unprepared students, he really seemed more interested in playing tennis and, especially, Ping-Pong (it is said that he always traveled with his paddles). He also painted well in the style of the Russian Wassily Kandinsky and other Viennese expressionists (Kandinsky and Schoenberg enjoyed a long personal friendship and professional relationship; Schoenberg's treatise *The Theory of Harmony* coincided exactly with the artist's *On the Spiritual in Art*. Moreover, the transformation of Schoenberg's music from the tonal to the atonal, first heard in his First String Quartet, parallels the transformation of Kandinsky's painting from the representational to the abstract). Schoenberg also wrote extensively, both plays and poems, as well as essays, about music, politics, and the social/historical situation of the Jewish people.

In 1945 the composer suffered a severe heart attack, and UCLA forced him to retire. His pension was $40.38 a month, laughably insufficient to support a family, so they all had to pitch in. Nevertheless, when he died on July 13, 1951, the family had to borrow money for the funeral.

Schoenberg suffered from triskaidekaphobia—fear of the number thirteen. He was born on the thirteenth of the month, which he always considered a portent. He feared turning seventy-six because the digits added up to thirteen. And he especially feared Friday, July 13, 1951, as it was the first Friday the thirteenth of his seventy-sixth year. Reportedly, he stayed in bed that day preparing for death. After begging her husband to quit this nonsense, to no avail, his wife, Gertrud, looked in on him late that night. She was, apparently, just in time to hear him utter his last word ("harmony") before dying. His time of death was 11:47 P.M., thirteen minutes before midnight on Friday the thirteenth.

◆◆◆◆◆◆◆

Somewhat more successful than Schoenberg at getting work within the film industry was his cousin Eric Zeisl, one of the youngest of the refugee composers. At least Zeisl had better luck dealing with MGM than Schoenberg did, contributing, along with émigré composer Bronislau Kaper and the Italian refugee composer Mario Castelnuovo-Tedesco, to the score for the studio's 1943 family classic starring the young Elizabeth Taylor and Roddy McDowell, *Lassie Come Home*. He later worked with Universal as well.

Zeisl was born in Vienna on May 18, 1905. His early career as a composer looked bright; in fact, his talent was respected enough to gain him entry to the prestigious Vienna Academy when he was only fourteen. Although he won the Austrian State Prize for Composition in 1934 (for a requiem), as with Schoenberg, his opportunities for a successful career evaporated when the Nazis took over Austria in 1938 and extended their ban on performances of music by Jewish composers.

On November 10, 1938, the day after the infamous *kristallnacht* when the Nazis destroyed Jewish shops and synagogues and began rounding up Jewish males, Zeisl and his wife, Gertrud, escaped on a train through Germany to France. The following year they emigrated to the United States, first settling in New York City before MGM lured them to Hollywood in 1941.

Eventually Hollywood politics—all his film music was uncredited—convinced Zeisl that working within the film industry was not for him, and he returned to serious composition, turning out, among others, a piano concerto and a cello concerto (for the celebrated émigré cellist Gregor Piatigorsky). His wife, Gertrud (trained as a lawyer), helped carry the family through hard times by teaching Latin and German. Zeisl died at the age of only fifty-three on February 18, 1959, after teaching his composition class at Los Angeles Community College, where one of his students was Jerry Goldsmith, who became famous with his scores for such films as *Lilies of the Fields, The Omen* (for which he won the 1976 Oscar), *Chinatown,* and *Patton.*

•••••••

Zeisl's composition class at Los Angeles Community College was soon taken over by one of the longest-lived of the émigré composers, Ernst Krenek, who died in Palm Springs at the age of eighty-four in 1984. But just because he lived the longest doesn't mean that he was the happiest.

Born in Vienna of Czech Catholic parents (his father was an army officer), Ernst showed an early aptitude for music. In 1920 he followed his composition teacher to Berlin, where he studied modern music (and also married and soon divorced Anna Mahler, the daughter of Alma and Gustav Mahler). He also discovered jazz and incorporated

Ernst Krenek's fame was based on his imaginative use of jazz in such operas as *Jonny spielt auf*, which was a huge success when it premiered at the Metropolitan Opera House in 1927. Less successful was his "spoken chorus" composition based on the station names in the Santa Fe Railroad timetable.

it into his first opera, 1923's *The Leap Over the Shadow*, before moving to Paris, then the center of jazz.

This passion of Krenek's would make him—at least at this point in his life—the most famous of all the future refugee composers. His 1927 opera *Jonny spielt auf* (*Johnny Plays On*), a jazz-based satire based on a book by Krenek about a black saxophonist, was a huge success in Leipzig, Germany. It brought the composer international fame when the work was presented by the Metropolitan Opera House in 1929, with the famous baritone Lawrence Tibbett portraying Jonny in blackface.

It should be remembered that much was being said—and done—with jazz at that time. In fact, the first talkie, *The Jazz Singer*, was released that year; Paul Whiteman's dance band was the most popular in the United States; and shortly Kurt Weill's bitter satire *The Three Penny Opera* would cause a storm when it opened in Berlin. The following year George Gershwin would write *An American in Paris*, which, like Krenek's *Jonny spielt auf*, incorporated street sounds. The jazz mania, in fact, went far deeper than performances and passions; according to some observers, it summed up an attitude toward life and social license. "Everything that appeals to our generation," the musicologist Alfred Einstein wrote, "finds its place in 'Jonny'; film, broadcasting, exoticism, luxurious hotels, motorcars, and trains."

In 1928 Krenek married actress Berta Haas, and five years later turned out his massive opera *Karl V*, commissioned by the Vienna Opera and composed in Schoenberg's twelve-tone system (it would not be premiered until 1938 in Prague). To the Nazis, however, Krenek was notorious as the composer of *Jonny spielt auf*, an opera that they had banned both because it was written by a Jew and because it starred a Negro. Ernst and Berta fled the day following the Anschluss and emigrated to the United States, where he taught in a number of conservatories, among them Hamline University in St. Paul, Minnesota, before settling in Los Angeles in 1947. It didn't work out at all as the couple had planned. In Hollywood, Krenek resented his life, hated having to teach know-nothings to make a living (often publicly belittling his students), and envied his more successful fellow composers. His marriage also fell apart, and after a divorce he married Gladys Nordenstrom, a former student.

Then matters improved—a little. In the early 1950s postwar Europe rediscovered him, and several of his operas were mounted, including *Pallas Athene weint*, a 1955 opus based on the death of Socrates, which Adlai Stevenson, the former Illinois governor, Democratic presidential candidate in 1952 and 1956, and United Nations ambassador, praised for its implied attack on McCarthyism. Krenek's new good fortune peaked with a 1960 production in Vienna of *Karl V*, twenty-seven years after he wrote it in the city, his election to the National Institute of Arts and Letters, and medals from the Austrian and Viennese governments.

Between royalties and his wife's salary teaching in the Los Angeles school district, the couple was able to buy a small home in Tujunga in California's San Fernando Valley. In 1966 they moved to Palm Springs in the desert Krenek loved.

Although Krenek left behind a huge amount of work, including over two hundred compositions and twenty books, not much of it is remembered today (however, a recording of *Jonny* was well received several years ago). Perhaps it was because he was *too* much of his time, following trends (jazz, twelve-tone music, etc.) instead of, like Schoenberg, being utterly and even arrogantly true to his convictions. A perfect example of this might be his "spoken chorus" called *The Santa Fe Timetable*, an a cappella work written in 1945. Seemingly inspired by what he called "the echolessnesses of the vast American expanses," it is based entirely on the station names along the route of the Santa Fe Railroad between Los Angeles and Albuquerque, New Mexico.

To put the futility of this in perspective, in the same year Krenek wrote the esoteric *Santa Fe Timetable*, Johnny Mercer and Harry Warren composed a similarly themed song for the Judy Garland movie

*The Harvey Girls.* The song, *On the Atchison, Topeka, and Santa Fe,* won the Oscar.

•••••••

Actually, the spoken chorus was invented by another refugee, Ernst Toch. He considered it a harmless diversion from his real vocation of composing serious music, yet his most popular work, composed in 1930, was the *Geographical Fugue.* It is written for four voices, each enunciating various cities, countries, and other geographic entities in precise contrapuntal fashion. The soprano's part goes, "Trinidad! And the big Mississippi and the town Honolulu and the lake Titicaca, the Popocatepetl is not in Canada, rather in Mexico, Mexico, Mexico! Canada, Malaga, Rimini, Brindisi . . . Yes Tibet, Tibet, Tibet . . . What to do to die today at a minute or two till two, A thing distinctly hard to say, yet harder to do . . ." John Cage, one of the high priests of modern music, was at the premiere in Berlin and is said to have been much taken with Toch's invention, traceable in the haphazardness that is more than evident in Cage's music.

Because of his book *The Shaping Forces in Music,* long a valuable music composition learning resource, Toch has always been considered a "musician's musician." Yet, unlike such rarified talents as others that term has been applied to, he, in fact, never took a composition class in his life and used Mozart's string quartets as models to teach himself how to write music. And although he would turn to Bach and others for "instruction," Mozart always remained the goal. Like many, he considered Mozart the greatest composer who ever lived. He once said, "If Mozart was possible, then the word 'impossible' should be eliminated from our vocabulary." Clearly, he taught himself well. Toch won the Mozart Prize awarded by the city of Frankfurt in 1909, Berlin's Mendelssohn Prize the following year, and the Austrian State Prize in composition four years in a row.

Born in Vienna in 1887, Toch was in the right place at the right time. Vienna was the center of the "new music" revolution that swept Europe after World War I (as well as the center for expressionism in art and writing, and the vastly influential "invention" of psychoanalysis by Vienna native Sigmund Freud). It was, in short, the center of an intellectual ferment.

Toch responded with an opera, *The Princess and the Pea* (based, of course, on the fairy tale, as was the much later musical *Once Upon a Mattress*, which made Carol Burnett a star). It premiered in 1927. In fact, Toch was considered to be one of the most important of the composers of the post-romantic style until, of course, the Nazis arrived. And, for Toch, they arrived in a dramatic fashion, with storm troopers stopping his opera *The Fan* in mid-rehearsal by storming the Cologne, Germany, concert hall in January 1933 and removing the baton from conductor William Steinberg's hand (Steinberg would later become music director of the Pittsburgh and Boston Symphony Orchestras, as well as the New York Philharmonic. Toch's publisher abandoned him; his works were burned; and the printing plates destroyed). Concerts of his music were canceled, and his name was added to the list of composers of "degenerate" music.

Toch quickly fled to Paris and signaled his wife Lilly and five-year-old daughter that the way was clear for them to come with a telegram that read, "I have my pencil." After a short stay in London, they emigrated to New York, where he taught for a time at the New School for Social Research (George Gershwin would help him straighten out some of his publishing problems). They soon moved to Los Angeles, where he taught at the University of Southern California and began composing again, both concert music and music for films, which would become a profitable side career.

For over a decade he composed film scores. Three of his films were nominated for Oscars, a record few film composers would equal (in 1936 for the Henry Hathaway–directed film *Peter Ibbetson*, starring

Gary Cooper; in 1941 for *Ladies in Retirement*; and in 1944 for *Address Unknown*). And in 1956 his serious compositions were rewarded when he won the Pulitzer Prize for his Third Symphony.

Along the way, Ernst Toch wrote other spoken choruses, including one based on cocktail-party conversations. Far more seriously, soon after arriving in Los Angeles, Toch composed the *Cantata of the Bitter Herbs*, a retelling of the Passover story as an appeal for universal justice and liberation from oppression (surely an appropriate subject at the time or, for that matter, at any time). Set to lush late-romantic music, the piece includes a quartet that has been likened to the beauty of the luminous trio at the close of Richard Strauss's opera *Der Rosenkavalier*. It was premiered in Los Angeles during World War II.

In 1948 Toch suffered a heart attack that caused him to reevaluate his lifework; the result was that he composed seven symphonies in a short period of time. In 1962 he finished his fourth opera, *The Last Tale*, adapted from *The Arabian Nights*. In Toch's ninety-minute work, Scheherazade is a member of a revolutionary movement aimed at overturning the corrupt sultan.

Unfortunately, Ernst Toch never saw the work staged, as he died on October 1, 1964. It would take more than a generation for *The Last Tale* to be finally mounted by the local Folk Theater in the Saxon town of Bautzen on November 18, 1995. It was well received, despite being produced in a location the Nazis had used as an internment camp, where the Tochs had lost family and friends in the Holocaust.

After moving to America, Toch would often refer to himself as the world's most forgotten composer. Nevertheless, he seemed, more than most, to maintain a sense of humor about himself. For a time he, his wife, and their friends would gather for informal parties at the Tochs' "Villa Majestic" on the beach in Santa Monica. It had been constructed of old shipping crates.

Jean Renoir (right), son of the renowned impressionist painter, was equally
famous as a filmmaker in golden-age Hollywood. He is here photographed
with a reporter on a set at Universal Pictures Studios.

# 18

······

# The French Arrive

## *Jean Renoir, René Clair, and Max Ophuls*

As noted elsewhere in this book, Jean Renoir, son of the great French impressionist painter Pierre-Auguste Renoir, helped Charles Laughton assemble a world-class art collection in his house in the Los Angeles suburb of Pacific Palisades. But as film fans know, Jean Renoir was far more than an art hound. He was, in fact, the greatest of the pre-new-wave French film directors. One of his movies, 1937's lyrically anti-war *The Grand Illusion*, made him internationally famous and, like its successor, 1939's *Rules of the Game* (*La Règle du Jeu*), a film about upper-class French society on the eve of World War II, is high on just about everyone's list of the greatest films ever made. Following the fall of France in 1941, he and fellow directors, including Max Ophuls and René Clair, fled to Hollywood.

Jean Renoir was born in the Montmartre section of Paris on September 15, 1894, the second son of the world-famous artist and his wife, Aline Victorine Charigot. When he was a child, his family bought a home in the south of France, where he spent much of his childhood immersed in the art world (Renoir painted his family several times, Jean memorably with his nanny) and acquiring a love of nature that was, of course, one of the hallmarks of his father's work. "In nature nothing is created, nothing is lost, everything is transformed," Jean once said. In 1913, after completing his studies at the university in Aix en Provence, he joined the army, where he served as a cavalryman and later as a pilot.

After reaching the rank of lieutenant, he was discharged because of a bullet wound in his thigh, which left him with a slight limp.

A year after his father's death in 1919, Jean—then pursuing a vocation as a ceramicist—married his father's model Andrée Heuchling, who later starred in a number of French films under the name of Catherine Hessling. Born in 1920, Heuchling is familiar to art lovers as the subject of Renoir's painting *Head of a Woman*.

Inspired especially by Charles Chaplin (who for years he knew of only by his French nickname "Charlot"), Jean Renoir had developed a love of film. Actually, in his 1974 autobiography, he says that it was his nanny, his mother's cousin Gabrielle Renard (with whom his father painted Jean as an infant), who first awoke his interest in film.

With inherited money he set up an independent production company and in 1924 directed his first film, *La Fille de L'eau* (released in America as *The Whirlpool of Fate*, the fully restored film was honored with a special eightieth-birthday presentation at the 2005 Cannes Film Festival). It starred Hessling in her first role, succeeded by starring roles in Renoir's next film, *Nana* (an adaptation of Zola's famous novel), and *Charleston*, an erotic fantasy made in 1927. With the coming of sound, the couple separated, and Renoir began a liaison with Marguerite Mathieu, a film editor who adopted his surname, although Renoir never married her.

Among Renoir's first talkies was 1932's *La Nuit du Carrefour* (*A Night at the Crossroads*), an adaptation of Georges Simenon's novel in which Renoir's older brother, Pierre, played Inspector Maigret. That year he also made *Boudu Sauve des Eaux* (*Boudu Saved from Drowning*), which was remade in 1986 in Hollywood as *Down and Out in Beverly Hills*. Like many artists and intellectuals of the era, Renoir was drawn to the struggles of the working class; in 1936 he acted on his beliefs by producing *La Vie Est a Nous* (released in English as *The People of France*) for the French Communist Party; the film would be restricted until government censors lifted a ban in 1969.

Based on Maxim Gorky's play *The Lower Depths*, *Les Bas-Fonds*, also made in 1936, marked Renoir's first collaboration with the great French actor Jean Gabin, the man who would star so memorably in *Grand Illusion*. "He is the most honest man I have ever known in my life," he once said. "Oh! Wait. I know one other honest person, Ingrid Bergman," Renoir added of the star with whom he made *Elena et Les Hommes* (*Elena and the Men*) twenty years later.

*Grand Illusion*, released in 1937, was immediately banned in Germany by Nazi propaganda boss Joseph Goebbels, who convinced the Italian government to ban it as well. This turned out to be rather embarassing for Mussolini's government when the film won the Venice Film Festival Best Artistic Ensemble Award. Based on a true story, the film's theme is the power of the camaraderie between soldiers, as well as the human passion for freedom, even in wartime. Erich von Stroheim, who had been working in Hollywood as a director since 1919 and had recently taken up acting, played the chivalrous, albeit by-the-book commandant of a prison fortress. Jean Gabin played a Jewish officer determined to escape.

Renoir, however, held no illusions about the power of film—at least the power of the many pacifist films made at the time—to change other aspects of human nature. When asked how much they may have affected history, he said, "In 1936, I made a picture named *La Grande Illusion,* in which I tried to express all my deep feelings for the cause of peace. This film was very successful. Three years later the war broke out. That is the only answer I can find."

The following year, 1938, brought another film based on a Zola novel and starring Gabin, *La Bête Humaine* (*The Human Beast*). It was followed by *Rules of the Game*, now recognized as a masterpiece, but at the time a commercial disaster. At one showing in 1939, a Paris audience, apparently infuriated by its gloominess and Renoir's satirical portrait of the French aristocracy, actually tried to destroy the seats in the theater. The film was banned by the government, and the original negative of the movie was destroyed in an air raid in 1942. It was not until the film was restored in 1959 that it began to be recognized as the landmark film it is . . . a biting look at the amorality of an entire generation that, perhaps, the first audiences chose not to see. Even Renoir, who appears in the film, wasn't very sure about what he had made. "During the shooting of the film I was torn between my desire to make a comedy of it and the wish to tell a tragic story," the director later said. One of the film's most famous sequences is a brutal "rabbit hunt," which parallels the superficial bourgeois partying.

When World War II broke out, the forty-five-year-old Renoir joined the film service of the French Army but, with the Nazi invasion and occupation of his country, was forced to flee to the United States. On March 8, 1941, a month after his arrival, he wrote his son, Alain (later a filmmaker), who was still in the defeated French Army, "I do not yet know all the possibilities of Hollywood, because it's a place where you never see anyone. I saw the heads of Fox one or two times for a few minutes and that was all. If there weren't such formalities over your visa and all the problems with the Bank and Taxes, which are very complicated, we would only see a few friends and that's all." In 1943 he married Dido Freire, his script girl.

Renoir's first Hollywood film was the anti-Nazi propaganda film *This Land Is Mine,* which starred Maureen O'Hara and Charles Laughton. Two years later Renoir made *The Southerner,* starring Zachary Scott; it is generally acknowledged to be his best American film and, other than *The Grapes of Wrath*, the best film about American labor. In all these films you see the poetic side of his philosophy of filmmaking. "I began to realize that the gesture of a laundress, of a woman combing her hair before a mirror, of a streethawker near a car, had an incomparable plastic eloquence," he once said of his evolution as a director.

In *The Southerner*, a story about a dirt-poor sharecropper and his family, he drew on the same poetic motivations. "What attracted me to the story was precisely the fact that there was no story, nothing but a series of strong impressions," he wrote in his autobiography *My Life in Films*, "the vast landscape, the simple aspiration of the hero, the heat and the hunger. Being forced to live a life restricted to their daily material needs, the characters attain a level of spirituality of which they themselves are unaware."

In 1951 Renoir went to India, where he made his first color film, *The River*, a meditative look at life in post-imperial India based on a Rumer Godden novel. He returned to Europe to make his next film, the first of three in which he indulged his lifelong life-as-theater obsession: *Le Carrosse d'Or* (*The Golden Coach*). Although it was not a commercial success, the film, based on the Italian *commedia dell'arte* tradition, remains a favorite of many film fans for its sumptuous beauty and its score, largely based on Vivaldi's music. Most of all, however, it gives film lovers the opportunity to see the great Anna Magnani, best known for her roles in Italian neo-realistic films, letting her hair down in a rare comedy role. The other two life-as-theater films were 1955's *French Cancan*—unlike *The Golden Coach*, this loving look at turn-of-the-century Paris was a huge success—and 1956's *Elena and Her Men*. Besides the appearance of Magnani, the trio of films showcased several other star turns, including that of Jean Gabin (in *French Cancan,* which also included an appearance by the unforgettable chanteuse Edith Piaf) and, as noted earlier, Ingrid Bergman as Elena.

His next films included *Le Testament du Docteur Cordelier* (*The Will of Dr. Cordelier*), an adaptation of Robert Louis Stevenson's *Dr. Jekyll and Mr. Hyde* starring Jean-Louis Barrault, made originally for television in 1961. The next year brought *Le Caporal Épinglé* (The Elusive Corporal), an attempt to return to the theme of freedom and personal dignity of *The Grand Illusion*. Renoir considered it as his "saddest film," but it proved less successful than it should have been because of poor editing, over which he had no control.

In 1975 Renoir received an honorary Oscar, and in 1977 he was made an officer of the French Legion of Honor. Besides his autobiography, he wrote a biography of his father in 1962, *Renoir, Mon Père* (*Renoir, My Father*).

Poet, humanist, genius—all are valid descriptions of Jean Renoir. And the wonderful thing about his body of work (for which he received that Oscar) is that all are apparent in most of his work, especially the immortal classic *The Grand Illusion*. Renoir died in Beverly Hills, California, on February 12, 1979.

••••••

Although Jean Renoir is today considered the greatest French director of his era, at the time the journalist-turned-filmmaker René Clair was thought of as the leading Gallic director. In 1957 André Bazin, co-founder of the influential film review *Cahiers du Cinéma*, who is generally considered the most important and influential film critic of the post–World War II era, wrote, "René Clair is probably, after Chaplin, the most esteemed director in the world." In 1962 Clair was elected to the French Academy, the first film director to receive this singular honor.

One reason for his fame was his ability to translate the light wit and elegance inherent in the concept of "Frenchness" into moving pictures. And, for the most part, it's all there in the seventy or so films he wrote, directed, or produced during his career. They range from farce to sentimetal comedy; among them are 1931's *À Nous la Liberté* (*Freedom for Us*), a satire on modernization that predated by five years—and may have partially inspired—Chaplin's similar *Modern Times*, and 1935's *The Ghost Goes West*, starring Robert Donat, Jean Peters, and Elsa Lanchester, which he also co-wrote. In 1942 he made the delightful *I Married a Witch*, with Fredric March, Veronica Lake, Robert Benchley, and Susan Hayward. René Clair also produced and directed the best of the four versions of Agatha Christie's mystery about ten people who are invited to a remote mansion only to be

René Clair with Marlene Dietrich on the set of *The Flame of New Orleans.* The most important film critic of the era called Clair "after Chaplin [probably] the most esteemed director in the world." The reason was his ability to distill a particularly French wit and elegance into his films, including *À Nous la Liberté,* which predated Chaplin's similar *Modern Times* by half a decade, and *Le Million*, which is said to have inspired the Marx Brothers' *A Night at the Opera*.

murdered one by one: 1945's *And Then There Were None*, starring Barry Fitzgerald, Walter Huston, and Dame Judith Anderson.

René Clair was born René-Lucien Chomette on November 11, 1898, in Paris. After working as a journalist, he soon discovered a passion for cinema while acting in some early French silents, and in 1924 he directed his first film, *Paris qui dort* (released in English as *The Crazy Ray*), a comic satire with a science-fiction twist. During the 1920s he also made some original films, including an avant-garde short, *Entr'acte* (with music by Erik Satie, the film features a chess game between Dadaist artists Man Ray and Marcel Duchamp), and the musicals *Sous Les Toits de Paris* (*Under the Roofs of Paris*, one of the first French films to use sound) and *Le Million*, about the search for a lottery ticket, said to have inspired the Marx Brothers' *A Night at the Opera*.

In the mid-1930s he first went to England, where he made one film (*The Ghost Goes West*, in 1935 for Alexander Korda) before moving on to Hollywood, where he remained throughout the war. There he make six films, including *I Married a Witch* and 1942's *Forever and a Day,* the story of an English mansion and its inhabitants from 1804 into World War II (a metaphor for England itself), with sections directed by seven directors, twenty-two screenwriters (including Christopher Isherwood), and one hundred stars, including Charles Laughton (as a tipsy butler), Laughton's wife Elsa Lanchester, Buster Keaton (as an assistant to the later knighted Cedric Hardwicke, who plays a plumber), Claude Rains, Merle Oberon, Ray Milland, and Ida Lupino. It sounds impossible, but somehow it works.

After World War II, Clair returned to France, where in 1947 he made *Le Silence Est d'Or* (*Silence Is Golden*), released in the United States as *Man About Town*. Starring Maurice Chevalier, like Renoir's *French Cancan*, it celebrated a long gone world from the filmmaker's distant past, the world of French silent filmmaking. *Le Silence Est d'Or* was fairly popular, but Clair's next films were less successful, among them a project that seemed to be a sure bet, 1952's *Les Belles de Nuit*

(*Beauties of the Night*), which starred Gérard Philipe, Martine Carol, and Gina Lollobrigida (then in her twenties).

René Clair died at the age of eighty-two in Neuilly-sur-Seine, France, on March 15, 1981.

•••••••

Max Ophuls was born Max Oppenheimer into a family of industrialists in the Saar region of Germany, but instead of joining the family business, as was expected of him, he became a theater critic and then a celebrated director of plays and operas. When talkies came on the scene, he immediately was attracted to the cinema, making his debut in 1932 with a film version of Smetana's opera *The Bartered Bride.*

Forced to leave Germany because of his Jewish background, he first moved to Paris, where in 1938 he drew on his German roots to make *Le Roman du Jeune Werther* (*The Romance of Young Werther*), an adaptation of Goethe's famous novel (as well as Massenet's equally famous opera). With the Nazi invasion and occupation of France, Ophuls was forced to flee again, this time to Hollywood. It took him some time to get up to speed in the American film capital because of the alien—to him—production system, but by 1947 he was making movies again. Among them were *The Exile* (a historical romp with Douglas Fairbanks, Jr., and Maria Montez), *Letter from an Unknown Woman* (1948, starring Joan Fontaine and Louis Jourdan), and a pair of films noir: *Caught* (with the young Barbara Bel Geddes, James Mason, and Robert Ryan) and *The Reckless Moment* (with James Mason and Joan Bennett), both made in 1949.

Ophuls then returned to France, where in 1950 he made one of his most successful films, *La Ronde*, based on Schnitzler's sexual romp and cast with some of the greatest French film actors of the era, including Simone Signoret, Jean-Louis Barrault, and Danielle Darrieux. Set in turn-of-the-century Vienna and featuring the lilting music of Oscar Strauss, it is an enchanting merry-go-round (*la ronde*) of a film. His

*Letter from an Unknown Woman* was the French émigré filmmaker Max Ophuls's American masterpiece. Here the director clowns around with Joan Fontaine on the 1948 set.

last film was 1955's *Lola Montès,* an early CinemaScope romantic drama starring Martine Carol and Peter Ustinov.

Two years later, on March 25, 1957, Ophuls died in Hamburg.

And there the story would end for many directors. But Max Ophuls was lucky . . . he had a son who would continue to work in film.

Marcel Ophuls, born in 1929, came with his father to Hollywood, where he attended high school. He went on to study at Occidental College in Los Angeles, as well as at the University of California at Berkeley and the Sorbonne in Paris. Moving back to France with his father in 1951, he became an assistant to filmmakers, including Anatole Litvak, and worked in German and French television. After a fairly inauspicious start, the younger Ophuls hit his stride with the four-and-a-half-hour film *The Sorrow and the Pity,* a chronicle of life in France during the Nazi occupation. From the day it opened in 1971, it has been hailed as one of the most influential movies of all time. Since then, Marcel Ophuls has continued making historical documentaries, including *Hotel Terminus: The Life and Times of Klaus Barbie,* which won the 1988 Oscar for Best Documentary.

Once called "the Olivier of the Orgasm" for the sexuality of her early films, the Austrian émigré Hedy Lamarr, here photographed at her Beverly Hills home, invented the technology that made the cellphone possible.

# 19

# Porn Star, Hollywood Legend, and Inventor

## *The Unlikely Career of Hedy Lamarr*

Say it's 1941, and as the storm clouds of war are gathering, someone suggests the following story idea to the production chief of a major Hollywood studio: "It's simple," says the hopeful screenwriter, encapsuling the story in the shorthand then and now preferred by the film capital's decision makers, "Gorgeous German-Jewish actress, trained in Germany's greatest acting school, becomes notorious as a porn star and a friend of both Hitler and Mussolini. Just before the war, she deserts her Nazi husband (a secret Jew and arms manufacturer), whom she loathes, by drugging the maid he hired to spy on her in her castle home, comes to Hollywood . . . becomes a superstar, and, on the side, patents a torpedo guidance system that could help win the war."

Despite the fact that the plot has everything—war, a hated marriage to an evil man, sex, a flight to freedom, a new life, and then potential revenge—even in that era of unabashedly patriotic films, no studio boss would buy such an outrageous idea. For one thing, few were prepared to believe that a woman—especially one famed as one of the most beautiful actresses in Hollywood—would have had the brains to invent such a technically advanced piece of electronic gear (or invent anything at all—Madame Curie, the discoverer of radium, was considered somewhat of a cultural aberration).

Yet, however unbelievable, the story is true and stands as one of the most remarkable among those of the Hollywood refugee and émigré population. So advanced was her invention that it actually formed the basis of much of modern communication, including cell phone and satellite communications technology. But the protagonist of the story also knew how Hollywood worked, keeping her ears and eyes wide-open while hiding a brilliant, inventive mind beneath one of Hollywood's most breathtakingly photogenic exteriors. She knew exactly how women, especially movie actresses, were stereotyped at the time, and she made it work for her. Her name was Hedy Lamarr, and as she once remarked, "Any girl can be glamorous. All she has to do is stand still and look stupid."

Hedy Lamarr was born near Vienna on November 19, 1913, as Hedwig Eva Maria Kiesler. During her teens she attended Max Reinhardt's famous acting school in Berlin. In 1932, still eighteen, she showed off what she had learned in the Czech film *Extase* (*Ecstasy*). In it, she plays a love-hungry young wife of an indifferent old husband and appears in a steamy love scene that shocked audiences for its animal passion. But that was nothing compared to the reaction over what else she showed off; in the movie she also bares her breasts and runs naked through the woods. It was the first fully nude shot in commercial film history.

Close-ups of her face simulating passion in the film, in fact, eventually brought her a somewhat equivocal designation as the "Laurence Olivier of Orgasm." Such acting—not to mention the nudity—was morally unacceptable, certainly in Hollywood, where only a few years earlier the scandalous behavior of a number of stars brought about self-censorship. Unsurprisingly, *Ecstasy* was banned in the United States for years on charges of indecency.

In 1933 her parents placed the young Hedwig into an arranged marriage with an Austrian armaments manufacturer named Friedrich "Fritz" Mandl. Like many in the arms business at the time, he had no compunction about violating international agreements and selling weapons to those otherwise prohibited from rearming by the Versailles Treaty. (After meeting Hedy, he reportedly spent three hundred thousand dollars—worth more than ten times that amount today—trying to buy up all the outstanding prints of *Ecstasy*.) Of course, to make his arms deals, Mandl had to entertain prospects, including Adolf Hitler and Benito Mussolini. And an important part of those business dinners was the presence of Mandl's gorgeous, and equally famous, wife to enchant the clients.

But as it turned out, while sipping endless crystal goblets of *sekt*, Hedy was doing more than just dazzling her husband's customers. She was listening to everything they were saying, as well as plotting how to get out of it all. Despite being married to one of the wealthiest men in the world, living in a castle in Salzburg (which a generation later would be one of the locations of the film version of *The Sound of Music*), and owning matchless jewels and the most expensive Mercedes money could buy, she was basically what is today described as a trophy wife—and she hated it. In 1937, after four years of marriage, she tried to escape.

The attempt was a failure, but it also produced one of the most famous anecdotes about Lamarr. As she was running, Mandl was so close on her heels that, at one point, she snuck into a brothel to hide (other stories claim it was a club that showed pornographic films, but may have hosted a brothel as well). In any event, when Mandl arrived, Hedy took refuge in one of the rooms. As the story goes, the male customer then arrived, and she was forced to have sex with him so her husband wouldn't recognize her when he broke in, searching for his wayward wife.

For her next attempt at escape, Hedy supposedly drugged the maid that Mandl had assigned to watch her (in the best cinemagraphic sleeping-pills-in-the-coffee style, naturally), put on a maid's uniform, and walked out the service entrance of the castle. She then made her way to London, where she acted in several plays, but more important for her future, met Louis B. Mayer, MGM's all-powerful boss. He immediately saw her potential and signed her to the standard seven-year contract aboard the French liner *Normandie*.

Because of the *Ecstasy* notoriety, Mayer insisted that she change her name. When the studio's famous press agent of the era, Howard Strickling, produced a list of acceptable names, she picked "Lamarr," an homage to Barbara LaMarr. The latter was a famously beautiful MGM star of the silent era who died of a drug overdose at the age of twenty-nine in 1926, the same year that her co-star in some lost dance films made in New York in 1914 also died: Rudolph Valentino. Discovered by Mayer, Douglas Fairbanks, Sr., and his wife Mary Pickford, the original LaMarr was not only celebrated as "the girl who is too beautiful," but she, like her namesake Hedy, possessed a razor-sharp intelligence and a wise, if not as bitter, understanding of human nature.

With her beauty, seductive, smoldering acting style, and the more or less personal sponsorship of Hollywood's most powerful studio boss, Hedy Lamarr could hardly fail in her new home. And she didn't.

Among Lamarr's Hollywood films were *White Cargo* and *Tortilla Flat*, both made in 1942, the latter based on the John Steinbeck novel. Her biggest success was clearly Cecil B. DeMille's *Samson and Delilah* (1949), in which Victor Mature rather laughably played the biblical strongman. It is said that DeMille had several reasons for making this addition to his biblical oeuvre: in Lamarr he had a woman he believed was beautiful enough to portray the seductress, and he finally had a use for the nineteen hundred peacock feathers he had gathered over the previous decade by chasing molting peacocks on his San Fernando Valley ranch—all of them were used in Lamarr's eighteen-foot train in the movie.

Sometime in the summer of 1940, Lamarr sought out a neighbor she had reverently met earlier at a party. George Antheil was an internationally known, albeit controversial, classical composer, who after his move to Hollywood a year or so earlier also worked as an opera and film composer (*Knock on Any Door, Tom Sawyer, The Fighting Kentuckian*). He also contributed a regular column to *Esquire* magazine on the war and, occasionally, on endocrinology, of all things. No one knows where he got his training, but in 1937 he had written a book on the subject called *Every Man His Own Detective: A Study of Glandular Endocrinology.* The reason Lamarr followed up on her intital meeting, according to several sources, was to ask him how she could enlarge the size of her breasts. As implants hadn't been invented yet, Antheil wasn't much help, and the conversation changed to a subject both had in common: the war in Europe, which would in a year and a half also involve America.

Although her former husband Mandl's firm specialized in shells and grenades, about the time he married Lamarr, he had begun manufacturing military aircraft, and one of the issues that occupied him was control systems. Mandl had been doing a lot of research in the field, and Lamarr heard it all at those dinners with arms buyers and began talking with Antheil about how to use what she had learned to control the torpedoes that were beginning to wreak havoc in the North Atlantic. To her, it seemed radio control was the way to go; all one had to do was jam a particular frequency, and the torpedo would be deflected from its target.

One afternoon Lamarr was sitting at Antheil's piano with the composer, who was idly hitting keys on the instrument, which she would then follow by banging on another note. Then her idea hit. As Antheil was changing the keys he was hitting, an idea occurred to Lamarr. As changing keys could change the music, could changing radio frequencies change or jam broadcast signals? The next day they sat on his floor and worked it out. Lamarr realized that the frequency of the signal controlling the torpedo needed to randomly change, so that any enemy attempt to block the signal would knock out only a small bit of the communication stream and have virtually no effect on its overall control. Thus, the concept known as "frequency hopping" was born.

How to get it to work was, of course, the question. Antheil offered a solution. Drawing from his 1926 *Ballet Mécanique,* scored for sixteen player pianos, all performing at the same time, he suggested using punched piano rolls to keep the radio transmitter and the torpedo receiver synchronized, allowing the signal to be broadcast over eighty-eight frequencies—one for each note on a piano keyboard. After spending several weeks working out the details, they sent the idea to the government. Under the direction of General Motors' then research director (later chairman) Charles Kettering, chairman of the National Inventors Council, the concept was improved, and patent 2,292,387 for a "Secret Communications System" was granted to Lamarr under her married name of the time, Hedy Kiesler Markey, on August 11, 1942.

But that was as far as it went. In that pre-transistor, pre-microchip era, it was simply too cumbersome to pack the vacuum tubes and associated technology into a torpedo—think putting a player piano into a missile. So the navy abandoned it, and Lamarr and Antheil dropped the matter. The actress directed her war efforts into selling war bonds (in one memorable night she sold $7 million in bonds at $25,000 a kiss), and George Antheil continued writing music.

But the "frequency hopping" concept wasn't forgotten. In 1957 Sylvania Electronics engineers made it a reality using the newly invented transistor, and five years later, after the Lamarr patent expired, frequency hopping was used by the United States to block communications during the Cuban missile crisis. The technology is now part of the Milstar defense communications systems, and is behind the latest in wireless Internet transmissions and cellular phones.

The rest of Hedy Lamarr's story isn't quite so happy. She never earned a nickel from her invention, which has made so many others millions of dollars. And as the movie industry changed to adapt to the television threat, her roles became fewer and fewer. Her last film was *The Female Animal* in 1958.

She was married and divorced six times. A year after she left Mandl, he left Germany for Buenos Aires and became an adviser to the country's dictator, Juan Perón, as well as a film producer, casting Perón's wife, Eva, in several of his films. Lamarr divorced Gene Markey, then a screenwriter, before the patent bearing his name was issued. He later married the owner of the celebrated thoroughbred horse farm in Kentucky, Calumet Farms.

From 1943 to 1947, Lamarr was married to the actor John Loder, followed by a two-year marriage to nightclub owner Ernest "Ted" Stauffer. In 1953 she married a Texas oilman named W. Howard Lee, who after they divorced in 1960, married the former film star Gene Tierney. Lamarr's last husband was Lewis J. Boies, a lawyer, whom she divorced in 1965, claiming that he had threatened her with a baseball bat.

In 1966 Hedy Lamarr was arrested for shoplifting at the May Company department store in Los Angeles, but was acquitted by a 10–2 vote in the subsequent jury trial. The bad publicity, coupled with her autobiography *Ecstasy and Me* (which was supposedly ghost-written and later disowned by Lamarr, who also denied some of the anecdotes surrounding her career), ended any chance of resuming an acting career.

Hedy Lamarr died at her home in Florida on January 19, 2000, and her ashes were scattered in the Vienna Woods near her birthplace. In 2003 the Boeing Company used her image in a series of recruitment ads featuring women in science. No mention of her acting career was made in them.

Peter Lorre, studying a script at his home in the 1940s, gave unforgettable performances in *Casablanca* and *The Maltese Falcon.* At his funeral in 1964 Vincent Price observed, "His voice, face, the way he moved [and] laughed [made him] the most identifiable actor I have ever known."

# 20

# The *Casablanca* Connection

## *Peter Lorre, Conrad Veidt, and Paul Henreid*

Casablanca has long been considered one of the greatest films ever made. It is also the ultimate refugee film, due in no small part to the casting from top to bottom. For the actors—not only those in *Casablanca*—that has occasionally been a mixed blessing. Some actors are so perfect for a role that they, often to their regret, become forever identified in the mind of the filmgoing public with a character or a type. Boris Karloff, for one. He was a fine actor who could turn in memorable performances in a variety of roles, but once he essayed the role of the Monster in director James Whale's *Frankenstein* in 1931, his legacy—despite making some two hundred films and over a hundred television guest appearances before his death in 1969—was defined by that single character. And, despite being Swedish-born, during the 1930s Warner Oland was totally identified with the wily Chinese film detective Charlie Chan. Closer to our own time, although he played other roles on-screen and onstage brilliantly, the late Christopher Reeve was, and probably always will be, Superman.

So powerful are the personalities and mannerisms of some actors that they can even outlive them. A perfect example is the refugee Jewish actor Peter Lorre, he of the big, sad eyes, chubby cheeks, and sinister, wheedling voice. Fans of classic movies remember him well for his performance as the spooky, sexually ambiguous Joe Cairo in *The Maltese Falcon* or the shady Ugarte in *Casablanca*. But those were only two of the movies in which his persona so embedded itself in our cultural consciousness that it was emulated in such popular icons as the *Looney Tunes* cartoons. Even now, more than forty years after his death, his unforgettable voice, look, and mannerisms are often emulated—obviously for their baleful effect—in both television and in movies. As one critic said, "Those marbly pupils in the pasty spherical face are like the eyes of a microscope through which you can see laid flat on the slide the entangled mind of a man." His unique delivery and character ensured a life for him long after he passed on.

It all obviously had to begin somewhere, and in the case of Lorre, that "somewhere" was Fritz Lang's 1931 iconic film noir *M*. In it he played a psychotic child killer, and the huge success of the movie gave him an international career. His characterization of the murderous Hans Beckert also created an entire genre of film characters. According to film expert Searle Kochberg of the London Jewish Cultural Center, *M* is not only a special work in its own right, but Lorre's persona in the movie also became the prototype of the weak, self-destructive man who became the central male character type in film noir. (Few know that about the time he was making *M*, Lorre was also playing a comic songster in *What Women Dream*, a film co-written in his Berlin years by another refugee who would attain the greatest heights in Hollywood, Billy Wilder. Had *M* not been released first, Lorre often speculated, he might have had a career as a screen entertainer.)

Peter Lorre was born Laszlo Loewenstein on June 26, 1904, to Alois and Elvira Loewenstein (rumored to be related to royalty) in the small mountain town of Rosenberg, then part of the Austro-Hungarian Empire and now Ruzomberok, Slovakia. When he was sixteen, he ran away from home and studied acting in Vienna, then made an acting debut in Zurich, Switzerland, where he also worked as a bank clerk, before settling in Berlin. There he worked with, as well as acted in plays by, a later Hollywood refugee, Bertolt Brecht, but otherwise went virtually unnoticed. Then he got his huge break when Fritz Lang cast him in *M*.

In another place or time, *M* would have made Lorre one of Europe's foremost film actors, but not an Austrian-Hungarian-German-Jew in Germany during the early 1930s. The Nazis' rise to power forced Lorre to flee to Vienna (on the same train, incidently, as fellow actor Oskar Homolka, director Josef von Sternberg, and violinist Jascha Heifetz); legend has it that Joseph Goebbels, Hitler's propaganda minister, personally warned him to leave. The following year Lorre got another break: a paid ticket to England to co-star as a charming, cunning villain in Alfred Hitchcock's first version of *The Man Who Knew Too Much.*

As the *Washington Post* pointed out in a 2002 homage, merely getting the part required no small acting prowess on Lorre's part. It recalled that Lorre had heard about Hitchcock's legendary storytelling abilities and once said, "So I used to watch him like a hawk and whenever I thought the end of a story was coming . . . I used to roar with laughter and somehow he got the impression that I spoke English." (The actor forced himself to learn most of his dialogue phonetically.) Based on an actual 1911 crime in London, *The Man Who Knew Too Much* was an international success, opening the door for Hitchcock's own move to Hollywood six years later. In 1956 the director would remake the movie with James Stewart and Doris Day; it would win the Best Song Oscar for Doris Day's number-one pop hit "Que Sera, Sera" ("What Will Be, Will Be").

In 1935 Lorre, now speaking English with the accent that was also part of his screen image, came to Hollywood, where he would continue playing wicked or wily foreigners. His first film in the movie capital, *Mad Love*, was of the wicked variety, in which he played a professor who surgically replaces the crushed hands of the pianist husband of the woman he loves with the hands of a guillotined murderer. That was succeeded by his starring role in Columbia Picture's 1935 production of *Crime and Punishment.* There is a particularly delicious anecdote associated with this film. The story goes that Lorre was determined to play the sociopath Raskolnikov in the film version of the Dostoyevsky novel, but was certain that Harry Cohn, boss of Lorre's studio, Columbia, would turn the project down if it were ever offered to him. So Lorre hired a secretary to type up a synopsis in words of one syllable and sent it over to Cohn. (It was generally agreed in Hollywood that Cohn was only semiliterate. This was not entirely true; however, it is a fact that, when challenged, he would often fail to spell the name of his studio correctly.)

Cohn loved the idea and green-lighted the project after first asking Lorre, "Tell me. Has the book got a publisher?" The film was directed by the imperious Josef von Sternberg, the Austrian-born, New York–raised director he met on the train out of Germany. Sternberg was already known for having cast Marlene Dietrich in *The Blue Angel* (1930), and he would go on to have a torrid relationship with the actress, as well as direct her in several more films.

Lorre's next project would make his name a household word in America—he was hired to star in 20th Century Fox's *Think Fast, Mr. Moto.* Based on John P. Marquand's Japanese detective, it was the first of a series of eight movies he made before worsening relations with Japan brought it to an end in 1939. Complete with Lorre donning steel-rimmed glasses and false buck teeth, it was designed to broaden the success of 20th's other "wily Asian detective" Charlie Chan series. In addition to making him famous, playing Mr. Moto worked wonders for Lorre himself. For years Lorre had been suffering from gallbladder problems, perhaps associated with a botched operation when he was living in Zurich years before, and to control the pain, he had become addicted to morphine long before he arrived in Hollywood. By this time he would often disappear between shoots on a film to indulge his addiction. After making the Mr. Moto series, he went into a sanitarium to overcome the habit and apparently remained free of the addiction for the rest of his life. (Ironically, Lorre played a drug addict in *The White Demon*, a film he made in Berlin just before starring in *M*.) The fame he gained from *Mr. Moto* set the stage for Lorre's greatest successes: Warner Bros.' *The Maltese Falcon* (made in 1941, the same year Lorre became a U.S. citizen) and the same studio's *Casablanca* (1942), teaming up with the likes of John Huston, Ingrid Bergman, Humphrey Bogart, and Sydney Greenstreet.

During the 1940s Lorre made a dozen and a half films (including Frank Capra's *Arsenic and Old Lace*, in which he first spoofed his screen persona, which he would do frequently in the future). In 1951 he returned to Germany to make *Der Verlorene* (*The Lost One*), which he co-wrote, directed, and starred in. Although it was critically acclaimed, the film, which examined the impact of World War II on ordinary Germans, did not prove popular in Europe, so Lorre returned to Hollywood to find work. There, with his fame slipping away (partly because the studios were wary of those who, like Lorre and *The Maltese Falcon* author Dashiell Hammett, were "greylisted" for their liberal beliefs), Peter Lorre morphed himself into a character actor, often continuing to spoof his sinister screen persona in television and feature films. One exception was his appearance as a clown in 1959's *The Big Circus*.

Lorre died of a stroke the year he made his last movie, Jerry Lewis's Chaplinesque *The Patsy* in 1964. At his funeral when his ashes were placed in a niche in the Cathedral Mausoleum at the Hollywood Memorial Cemetery, his friend Vincent Price (who also became famous for his creepy characters) said in the eulogy, "His voice, face, the way he moved [and] laughed [made him] the most identifiable actor I have ever known." Earlier he had observed, "Peter held back none of himself."

He didn't need to mention a familiar anecdote of the time. When Lorre and Vincent Price went to view Bela Lugosi at the actor's funeral in 1956, Lorre took one look at Bela, who was dressed in his famous Dracula cape, and quipped, "Do you think we should drive a stake through his heart—just in case?"

Lorre and his wife, Anna Marie, had one child, Catherine, born in 1950. In a really weird coincidence—certainly when one considers Peter Lorre's first big role—his daughter Catherine was abducted by the Hillside Stranglers, Kenneth Bianchi and Angelo Buono, who in two months in 1977 abducted and murdered ten women in Los Angeles. They let her go when they discovered she was Peter Lorre's daughter.

It is a fascinating fact that a number of the refugees who came to Los Angeles appeared with Lorre in *Casablanca*. Fascinating, but not entirely surprising, because the casting of Warner Bros.' Oscar-winning anti-war classic—considered by film scholar Leonard Matlin "the greatest Hollywood movie of all time"—occurred more or less at the same time as the greatest influx of refugees from Nazism. This obviously facilitated the film's casting enormously . . . in fact, of all the featured players in the film who get screen credit, only three were born in the United States. The presence of so many refugees heightened the intensity of the performances—credited and uncredited—in the movie. In the famous scene where the French national anthem, "La Marseillaise," is sung by a lone man (followed by others) over the German song "The Watch on the Rhine," many of the extras had real tears in their eyes; many were actual refugees from Nazi persecution in Germany and elsewhere in Europe and were overcome by the emotions the scene brought out. (Opera lovers of a certain age will notice a famous non-refugee in the crowd: the twenty-two-year-old Canadian bass-baritone George London.)

◆◆◆◆◆◆

And that brings us to the next of our *Casablanca* refugees, the man who first sings "La Marseillaise," Paul Henreid. In *Casablanca*, as many film fans know, Henreid plays a French Resistance leader, Victor Laszlo, who is married to Ilsa, the character immortalized by Ingrid Bergman. Because of Hollywood's puritanical and political standards of the time, when Bergman and Humphrey Bogart have their "we'll always have Paris" romance, Ilsa believes Laszlo is dead.

Paul Henreid, shown here with three admirers at a Hollywood cocktail party, was one of Hollywood's most dashing actors. After making nearly fifty films, he went on to become a television director, helming many episodes of *Bonanza*, *Maverick*, and *Alfred Hitchcock Presents*. Nevertheless, it would be the role of *Casablanca's* French Resistance leader Victor Laszlo that would immortalize his memory.

Ironically, when Henreid learned that he was being loaned by his studio, Selznick International, to Warner's to play Laszlo, he didn't want anything to do with it. Playing a secondary character in the film would, he believed, ruin a Hollywood career playing "continental lover" leads. And he was not entirely wrong, having just completed such a role in *Now, Voyager* (1942) in which he famously lit two cigarettes at once to comfort his distraught co-star, Bette Davis. In fact, his autobiography (co-written with Julius Fast), originally titled *Naked in Four Countries*, was published in 1984 as *Ladies' Man*. But like many Hollywood plans, it was all for naught: Although Henreid would make nearly fifty films (his last role was the Cardinal in 1977's *Exorcist II: The Heretic*) and direct extensively, it was, of course, the role of Victor Laszlo that immortalized him.

Paul Henreid was born Paul Georg Julius Hernreid Ritter Von Wassel-Waldingau on January 10, 1908, in Trieste, Italy, then part of the Austro-Hungarian Empire. Acting under the name of Paul von Hernried (also used in several of his early films), Henreid began his acting career studying at Max Reinhardt's theater school in Vienna. His subsequent refusal to join the Nazi Actor's Guild ended any chance for a German career, and he moved to London where, for a time, he was a popular stage actor. When anti-German feelings mounted in England in the late 1930s, Henreid accepted an offer to do a play in New York; the play fell through after his arrival, so he went on to Hollywood.

Among his Hollywood films was 1944's *The Conspirators*, which reunited him with his *Casablanca* co-stars Sydney Greenstreet and Peter Lorre. That same year he also played himself in *Hollywood Canteen*, along with such major stars as Bette Davis, Jack Benny, Joan Crawford, and Eddie Cantor. The year 1946 brought *Devotion*, in which he appeared with Ida Lupino and Olivia de Havilland, and a remake of the Somerset Maugham novel *Of Human Bondage* (with original music by fellow refugee Erich Korngold). His next major film was the noir thriller *Hollow Triumph*, which he also produced.

During the 1950s the actor would more or less exclusively spend his time on the other side of the camera lens, directing, among dozens of shows, *Bonanza*, *Maverick*, *The Big Valley*, and twenty-eight episodes of the *Alfred Hitchcock Presents* series. In 1964 he returned to the screen in the noir film *Dead Ringer* with his *Now, Voyager* co-star Bette Davis and his actress daughter, Monica Henreid, in a small role as a maid.

Paul Henreid died of pneumonia in Santa Monica, California, on March 29, 1992. Because of his double career—acting and directing—he is one of the very few Hollywood professionals to have two stars on the Walk of Fame.

◆◆◆◆◆◆◆

Elsewhere in this book we commented on what many people feel was deplorable judgment on the part of actor Werner Klemperer, son of the Jewish conductor Otto Klemperer, who fled the Nazis in 1933 to play the role of a comedic Nazi prison camp commander in the television series *Hogan's Heroes*. There is no such problem with the actor who was cast as the Gestapo Major Strasser in *Casablanca* . . . at $25,000 for five weeks' work, he was also the highest-paid actor on the set: Conrad Veidt. (The actor and future director Otto Preminger was Warner's first choice for the role; however, Darryl Zanuck, boss of 20th Century Fox, wanted $7,000 weekly to loan him out, and that was thought to be an outrageous sum. Ingrid Bergman, also contracted to 20th Century Fox, was paid the same $25,000, but for more weeks. The weekly salaries for other leads were: Humphrey Bogart, $2,200; Sydney Greenstreet, $3,750; Claude Rains, $4,000; and Peter Lorre, $1,750.)

Before fleeing Germany in 1933 with his third wife, Ilona (Lilli), Veidt was well-known, at least in the theatrical and film communities, for his hatred of the Nazis. In fact, according to a story at the time, he fled Germany for London just ahead of a Nazi death squad dispatched to silence him. (His first wife was Jewish, and whenever he had to

Less than a decade after Conrad Veidt and his wife fled his native Germany (and a Nazi death squad) in 1933, he was cast—unforgettably—as the Gestapo Major Strasser in 1942's *Casablanca*. The role would be the penultimate one for the Berlin-born actor, who died in Los Angeles the following year.

indicate his ethnic background on job forms, he would always write "Jewish.") He and his second wife, Felizitas Radke, married in 1923 and had a daughter, Viola. He married Ilona Prager a month before the couple was to flee Germany. They soon came to Hollywood, where Veidt had spent a productive three years in the late 1920s.

Hans Walter Conrad Weidt was born on January 22, 1893, in the Potsdam suburb of Berlin. His father, Philip, was a former military man turned conservative civil servant, and his mother, Amalie, brought up her son on a diet of adventure stories and fairy tales. In later years, his film career established, Veidt would often recall a trip when his mother took him to downtown Berlin (by horse-drawn streetcar), where they lunched and saw two early films. He was enchanted.

He attended school in the Schoenberg district of the German capital, graduating in 1912, last in his class of thirteen. He received his training, as did so many of the German-speaking Hollywood refugees, under the great Max Reinhardt, during which he adopted his trademark monocle (he had poor eyesight in his right eye and thought a monocle would add distinction).

During his career in Germany he played many roles, including Lord Nelson in 1921's *Lady Hamilton* and Rasputin in a 1930 film. But his work from this time is perhaps best remembered for his performances in the 1920 expressionist film *The Cabinet of Dr. Caligari* (another precursor of film noir) and, during a three-year stay in Hollywood (1926–29), *The Man Who Laughs*, based on a Victor Hugo novel. His character, who has a deformity that causes him to always smile, was, according to *Batman* cartoon creator Bob Kane, the inspiration for his supervillain The Joker. (In 1931 Universal Studios president Carl Laemmle wanted Veidt to play Dracula, but Bela Lugosi, who had played Dracula on Broadway and the West Coast, finally ended up with the movie role after the other choice, Lon Chaney, Sr., died in 1930. A hit for Laemmle's studio, the film launched Lugosi's long career playing in horror movies.)

In London, Veidt made such films as *The Spy in Black* (1939) and, the following year, *Contraband* and *The Thief of Bagdad* (his only color film, made in London and Hollywood, which he had earlier visited in 1926 when he co-starred with John Barrymore in *The Beloved Rogue*). In Hollywood, besides *Casablanca*, he made *A Woman's Face* with Joan Crawford (1941), the propaganda film *Nazi Agent*, and *All Through the Night* with his *Casablanca* co-star Humphrey Bogart, both in 1942.

After *Casablanca*, Conrad Veidt made only one more film, 1943's *Above Suspicion*, again with Joan Crawford (and Fred MacMurray). Veidt liked fast cars, gardening, swimming, and golfing; sadly, it was while playing a round of the latter on a Los Angeles golf course that he died on April 3, 1943, of a heart attack. Because he had been blacklisted in Nazi Germany, there was no official announcement there of his death. . . . Felizitas, and his daughter, Viola, heard about his death on the radio in Switzerland.

# Selected Bibliography

Agus, Ayke. *Heifetz As I Knew Him*. Amadeus Press/Hal Leonard, 2005.

Allen, Frederick Lewis. *Since Yesterday, 1929–1939*. Bantam, 1940.

Anderson, Clinton A. *Hollywood Is My Beat*. Prentice Hall, 1960.

Anger, Kenneth. *Hollywood Babylon*. Self-published (Phoenix: Associated Professional Services), 1965.

Auden, W. H. *Forewords and Afterwords*. Vintage, 1990.

————. *Collected Poems*. Vintage, 1990.

Bacall, Lauren. *Lauren Bacall: By Myself*. Knopf, 1978.

Bainbridge, John. *Garbo*. Holt, Rinehart and Winston, 1951.

Beauchamp, Cari. *Without Lying Down*. University of California Press, 1997.

Bedford, Sybille. *Huxley: A Biography*. Knopf/Harper and Row, 1974.

Berry, Sarah. *Screen Styles in 1930s Hollywood*. University of Minnesota Press, 2000.

Buckle, Richard. *Nijinsky*. Avon, 1971.

Burk, Margaret, and Hudson, Gary. *Final Curtain*. Seven Locks Press, 1996.

Callow, Simon. *Charles Laughton: A Difficult Actor*. Grove/Atlantic, 1988.

Chandler, Charlotte. *Nobody's Perfect: Billy Wilder, a Personal Biography*. Simon and Schuster, 2002.

Craft, Robert. *Stravinsky: Glimpses of a Life*. Knopf, 1993.

Dardis, Tom. *Some Time in the Sun*. Scribner, 1976.

Davie, Michael. *California: The Vanishing Dream*. Dodd, Mead, 1972.

Davies, Marios. *The Times We Had*. Ballantine, 1975.

Davis, Peter G. *The American Opera Singer*. Anchor, 1997.

De la Grange, Henri-Louis. *Mahler*. Doubleday, 1973.

DeMille, C. B. *Autobiography*. Prentice Hall, 1951.

Dunaway, David K. *Huxley in Hollywood*. Anchor, 1991.

Finch, Christopher, and Rosenkranz, Linda. *Gone Hollywood*. Doubleday, 1979.

Fine, David. *Imagining Los Angeles: A City in Fiction*. University of New Mexico Press, 2000.

Friedrich, Otto. *City of Nets*. University of California Press, 1986.

Gabler, Neal. *An Empire of Their Own*. Anchor/Doubleday, 1988.

Gallaz, Christophe. *Stravinsky*. Creative Education, 1993.

Gebhard, David, and von Breton, Harriette. *Los Angeles in the Thirties*. Hennessey and Ingalls, 1989.

Gibberd, Vernon. *Architecture Source Book*. Wellfleet, 1988.

Goodman, Ezra. *The Fifty-Year Decline and Fall of Hollywood*. Simon and Schuster, 1961.

Gordon, William A. *The Ultimate Hollywood Tour Book*. North Ridge Press, 2002.

Graham, Sheilah. *Confessions of a Hollywood Columnist*. Morrow, 1969.

Hadleigh, Boze. *Hollywood Gays*. Barricade, 1996.

Harmetz, Aljean. *The Making of "Casablanca"—Bogart, Bacall and World War II*. Hyperion, 2002.

Higham, Charles. *C. B. DeMille*. Scribner, 1973.

Higham, Charles. *Charles Laughton: An Intimate Biography*. Doubleday, 1976.

Hopper, Hedda. *From Under My Hat*. Macfadden, 1963.

Huxley, Aldous (Bridgeman, Jacqueline, ed.). *Huxley and God*. Harper Collins, 1992.

Isherwood, Christopher. *Christopher and His Kind, 1929–1939*. Farrar, Straus, 1976.

———. *Diaries, 1939–1960*. Harper Collins, 1996.

———. *Lost Years: A Memoir 1945–1951*. Harper Collins, 2000.

Jacobson, Laurie. *Hollywood Heartbreak*. Fireside/Simon and Schuster, 1984.

Johnson, Paul. *Modern Times: The World from the Twenties to the Eighties*. Harper and Row, 1983.

Kanin, Garson. *Moviola*. Pocket Books, 1979.

Keegan, Susanne. *Bride of the Wind: The Life of Alma Mahler*. Viking/Penguin, 1991.

Koch, Howard. *"Casablanca," Script and Legend*. Overlook, 1973.

Kurtzke, Herman. *Thomas Mann: Life as a Work of Art*. Princeton University Press, 2002.

Lamarr, Hedy. *Ecstasy and Me: My Life*. Bartholomew House, 1966.

Lamprecht, Barbara. *Richard Neutra*. Taschen, 2000.

Lanchester, Elsa. *Elsa Lanchester, Herself*. St. Martin's, 1983.

Lockwood, Charles. *Dream Palaces: Hollywood at Home*. Viking, 1981.

Loos, Anita. *Kiss Hollywood Goodbye*. Viking, 1974.

Madsen, Axel. *The Sewing Circle*. Birch Lane, 1995.

Mann, Erika. *The Last Year of Thomas Mann*. Farrar, Straus, 1958.

Mann, Katia. *Unwritten Memoirs*. Borzoi, 1975.

Mann, William J. *Wiseacre: The Life and Times of William Haines, Hollywood's First Gay Star*. Penguin, 1998.

McClellan, Diana. *The Girls*. LA Weekly Books/St. Martin's Press, 2000.

Merrill-Mirsky, Carol. *Exiles in Paradise* (catalog of the Hollywood Bowl Museum).

Monson, Karen. *Alma Mahler: Muse to Genius*. Houghton Mifflin, 1983.

Murray, Nicholas. *Aldous Huxley*. Thomas Dunne, 2003.

Neutra, Richard. *Survival Through Design*. Oxford University Press, 1954.

Preminger, Otto. *An Autobiography*. Bantam, 1978.

Reinhardt, Gottfried. *The Genius: A Memoir of Max Reinhardt*. Knopf, 1979.

Renoir, Jean. *My Life and My Films*. Scribner, 1974.

Rogers St. Johns, Adela. *Love Laughter and Tears: My Hollywood Story*. Doubleday, 1978.

Rooney, Mickey. *An Autobiography*. Putnam, 1965.

Russo, Vito. *The Celluloid Closet*. Harper and Row, 1987.

Schatz, Thomas. *The Genius of the System: Hollywood Filmmaking in the Studio Era*. Metro/Henry Holt, 1988.

Schnauber, Charles. *Hollywood Haven*. Ariadne, 1992.

Silvester, Christopher, ed. *Hollywood*. Grove, 1998.

Starr, Kevin. *Inventing the Dream*. Oxford University Press, 1985.

———. *Material Dreams*. Oxford University Press, 1990.

Steele, James. *R. M. Schindler*. Taschen, 1999.

Stravinsky, Igor (Robert Craft, ed.). *Selected Correspondence*. Knopf, 1982.

Stravinsky, Vera. *Dearest Bubushkin: The Correspondence of Vera and Igor Stravinsky, 1921–1954.* Thames and Hudson, 1985.

Thomson, David. *Beneath Mulholland: Thoughts on Hollywood and Its Ghosts.* Vintage, 1997.

Torrence, Bruce T. *Hollywood: The First Hundred Years.* New York Zoetrope, 1982.

Vieira, Mark A. *Greta Garbo: A Cinematic Legacy.* Abrams, 2006.

Viertel, Salka. *The Kindness of Strangers.* Holt, Rinehart and Winston, 1969.

Wallace, David. *Lost Hollywood.* St. Martin's, 2000.

———. *Dream Palaces of Hollywood's Golden Age.* Abrams, 2006.

———. *Hollywoodland.* St. Martin's, 2002.

———. *Malibu: A Century of Living by the Sea* (foreword). Abrams, 2005.

Walter, Bruno. *Of Music and Music Making.* W. W. Norton, 1961.

Wilson, Edmund. *The Twenties.* Farrar, Straus, 1979.

———. *The Thirties.* Farrar, Straus, 1980.

Zolotow, Maurice. *Billy Wilder in Hollywood.* Limelight/Hal Leonard, 2004.

# Index of Names

# Index of Films and Television Series